Ophelia
Thinks Harder

By

Jean Betts
&
Wm. Shakespeare

Laborious learning or painful pondering,
even if a woman should greatly succeed in it,
destroy the merits that are proper to her sex

- Kant

{The Play Press}

{The Play Press}

Ophelia Thinks Harder by Jean Betts
Revenge of the Amazons by Jean Betts
Camelot School by Jean Betts
The Misandrist by Jean Betts
Fold by Jo Randerson
shudder by Pip Hall
Mapaki by Dianna Fuemana
Frangipani Perfume by Makerita Urale
Fresh off the Boat by Oscar Kightley and Simon Small
Horseplay by Ken Duncum (with VUP)
Trick of the Light by Ken Duncum (with VUP)
Flipside by Ken Duncum (with VUP)
The Collective by Jean Betts (based on "Brecht & Co." by John Fuegi)
Baghdad, Baby! by Dean Parker
Awhi Tapu by Albert Belz
The Cape by Vivienne Plumb
The Mall by Thomas Sainsbury
Kikia Te Poa by Matthew Saville
Sit On It by Georgina Titheridge
The Christmas Monologues by Thomas Sainsbury
Me & Robert McKee by Greg McGee

Special thanks to -
Betts family, Circa Theatre, Shakespeare and original cast and crew.

Permission to perform these plays must be obtained from
Playmarket
P.O. Box 9767, Wellington, New Zealand
info@playmarket.org.nz

© Jean Betts
ISBN: 095-83393-2-5 : 978-0-958339-32-2

First published 1994 by The Women's Play Press with assistance from the Literature programme of the Arts Council of New Zealand

Printed by Printlink

Cover design by Joe Bleakley
Fifth reprint 2011 by {The Play Press}
P.O. Box 27 436, Wellington, New Zealand
stuff@playpress.co.nz   www.playpress.co.nz

First Production

Ophelia Thinks Harder was first performed at Circa Theatre, Wellington, on October 14ᵗʰ 1993, as part of a festival of new plays by women marking New Zealand's women's suffrage centenary. The cast were:-

Ophelia	Carol Smith
Maid	Perry Piercy
Hamlet	Steven Lovatt
Horatio	Joe Conway
Queen	Kate Harcourt
Rosencrantz	Carmel McGlone
Guildenstern	Lorae Parry
Polonius/Laertes	Mick Rose
Player 4	Charlie Bleakley
King	Nick Wyatt

Lighting design, operation (and Virgin Mary) – Emma Muir
Directed by Jean Betts
Designed by Joe Bleakley

The Virgin Mary does not need to be seen, but she needs a clear 'position' at least, so that when **Ophelia** speaks to her it is obvious immediately who she is addressing. Our lighting box was in a convenient position, so we dressed our operator in a blue towel and halo. One production had an appropriate icon hanging from the ceiling.

The **King** can be played by a dummy, who can be manipulated by the **Queen**.

Rosencrantz and **Guildenstern** were actually played by Digger and Nudger, the well-known male alter egos of two Wellington comediennes (Parry and McGlone). They are two ordinary kiwi blokes anxious to improve themselves by attending courses such as 'How to Find the Woman Within' – hence their suitability for the particular responsibilities of their (re-written) roles. This led to a fascinating twist at the end when **R&G** revert to women's clothing; in the same moment we were faced with Digger and Nudger cross dressing, while aware that the actors *were* actually women.

We decided that Dig and Nudge had had minimal acting experience, so they were often awkward and over excited, and sometimes unsure of their lines. They were occasionally alarmed when other characters had to push them around, or yell at them (I have retained some stage directions and script peculiarities which reflect this).

With a larger cast it is possible to place the interval after Scene 5, rather than after Scene 4, where we had to place it to allow for costumes changes. We had a minimal set (two strange beds) and the costumes were as fantastical as we could manage and ranged over the centuries as we saw fit. I feel it is important not to allow the audience to set the play in any particular place or time. Keeps them on their toes.

Writer's Note

The seeds of this play were sown when during an acting class, tutors expressed surprise that I had made Hamlet 'a believable woman' when delivering one of his famous soliloquies as an exercise. Why the surprise, I thought? Why the difficulty accepting that women (and actresses?) are capable of experiencing and expressing **Hamlet's** complexities?

It is unfortunate that in the magnificent old classics which reign supreme in our collective theatrical subconscious, the fascinating, complex, tortured, passionate, angst-ridden, cosmos-questioning and deeply funny characters are almost always male. By pushing feminism and humour into bed together, I aim not merely to entertain but to meddle ruthlessly with this subconscious. Too many of us still have difficulty accepting that women are as capable as men of these 'male' attributes and qualities, and I hope this play helps to dismantle some of the foundations of this deeply buried prejudice.

The answer was not to cast a woman as Hamlet yet again, but to explore Ophelia; to 'let her come in', and 'strew dangerous conjectures in ill breeding minds'. After all, she has at least as much reason as Hamlet to rage and despair. Her culture forces her into a boring and pointless existence, reinforced by her bossy brother and father. She has to adjust to the loss of both parents (eventually), and cope with cruelly dismissive behaviour from her boyfriend. So she is a complex, confused, intelligent, moody and passionate creature in her own right.

I remembered studying **Hamlet** at school, and like most other girls in my class, identifying with him and finding **Ophelia** alien; while at the same time being aware that even so, too often in my life I was judged not on how I measured up to **Hamlet**, but on how I compared to **Ophelia**. Few boys experience this trauma. It isn't fair. I dedicate this play to all girls who felt, and feel, the same.

Jean Betts

P.S.

Many of the misogynistic quotes and religious facts in the play may seem appalling and absurd; but they are all, astoundingly, direct quotes from various saints and historians.

"For the myths of the East, the myths of the West, the myths of men and the myths of women – these have so saturated our consciousness that truthful contact between nations and lovers can only be the result of heroic effort. Those who prefer to bypass the work involved will remain in a world of surfaces, misperceptions running rampant."

David Henry Hwang (from afterword to *M. Butterfly)*

Characters

The play is written for the minimum cast of 9, as below, and allows for the frequent costume changes required.

Subsequent productions have had casts of between 14 and 30, allowing one part per person, multiple Ophelias, extra court members and occasionally onstage armies.

Ophelia

Maid — and Player Lover

Hamlet

Horatio — and Player Mother

Queen — and Woman 2

Rosencrantz (female) — and Woman 1
Player 2
St Joan

Guildenstern (female) — and Player 3
Ophelia's Mother

Polonius/Laertes — and Player 1
Player Father
Woman 3

Player 4 (a boy about 12 years old)

(King – optional)

(Virgin Mary – optional)

Gertrude   *I will not speak with her.*

Gent   *She is importunate, indeed, distract.*
Her mood will needs be pitied.

Gertrude   *What would she have?*

Gent   *She speaks much of her father; says she hears*
There's tricks i' th' world, and hems, and beats her heart;
Spurns enviously at straws; speaks things in doubt,
That carry but half sense. Her speech is nothing,
Yet the unshaped use of it doth move
The heavens to collection; they yawn at it,
And botch the words up fit to their own thoughts;
Which, as her winks and nods and gestures yield them,
Though nothing sure, yet much unhappily.

Horatio   *Twere good she were spoken with; for she may strew*
Dangerous conjectures in ill breeding minds

Gertrude   *Let her come in.*

Hamlet, Act IV Sc 5

Ophelia
Thinks Harder

———

Scene 1

*The Castle. On one side is **Ophelia**'s area – bed, books, clothes. On another is an area with a bed for the **Queen**, perhaps. Otherwise maybe the odd chair.*

*During ominous introductory music, the **Maid** enters and performs a quiet pagan ritual over two boxes, with candles, water and herbs. She looks very ragged and tired.*

***Ophelia** can be seen to one side, apparently praying. She wears black; a black dress (it must be a dress or skirt, as you will see) including a hat with a sort of veil, variously up and down. We will soon realise she has been praying to the **Virgin Mary**, whose 'position' should be established at this point for the rest of the play. She seems anxious. She eventually notices the **Maid**, and rushes over upsetting a quiet incantation.*

Ophelia Is it time?

Maid The stars are favourable. *(She shows alarm at **Ophelia**'s scant respect for the ritual)*

Ophelia *(Inspecting onions in first box)* None of them has sprouted, not one. You said one of them would sprout! *(Inspecting snails in second box)* And all the snails are dead. *(Rattles the box)* Every one.

Maid But the slime, Madam, read the slime.

Ophelia The slime. Phew. Well, there's plenty of slime. But I can't make out one initial. Mind you, if you wanted to, you could see the whole alphabet. There – that could be an H – or an I. Or even an Z – or an N... Oh this is pointless, girl.

(She kicks her) Is there nothing I can do to find out what lies ahead? Who lies in store for me? There must be something I can do apart from just wait, wait, wait ...

Maid Patience, Madam ...

Ophelia Aaargh! I want to make things *happen!*

Maid There is a divinity which shapes our ends, rough hew them how we will ...

Ophelia Fool, I only want to help make happen what's going to happen anyway. If I knew my fate; if I was sure of his name, I could avoid all the doubts and confusions and embarrassments ... save so much *time* ...!

Maid Madam, I see a Q!

Ophelia Q? I know no Qs. And even if I did, what would I do? Pace the floor until he happened to see *my* initial in an onion? Sit like patience on a monument?

Maid Madam, there is much that can be done ...

Ophelia Oh I give up. What's the point in doing anything? I'm just going to give up, and sit here for the rest of my life, and be – bewildered. It's the only honest existence. The world's a prison.

> *The **Maid** furtively reveals a small, distinctive phial of bright red potion. Maybe there is a little jangly magic-music to emphasise its power.*

Ophelia Now what?

Maid Madam, this is very powerful magic; a most dangerous potion - it must only be used as a last resort. One drop of this in contact with the skin will make man or woman madly dote upon the next live creature that it sees.

Ophelia Madly dote?

Maid Helplessly in love.

Ophelia Live creature. Dog? Goldfish? *(She smells it)* Phew! What's in it?

Maid Spawn of a frog that's been steeped in hellebore – semen of a bull collected after copulation, blood of worms, faeces of sheep and ...

Ophelia Uggh! Is this a love potion or a curse?

Maid True – the recipes are very similar ...

Ophelia Hmm. Sounds a bit hit and miss. You'll have to be a last resort, poison of Cupid *(She throws the phial down)* Oh, tomorrow and tomorrow and tomorrow creeps in this pretty pace from day to day ...

> ***Hamlet** crashes in, very agitated*

Hamlet Ophelia!

> ***Ophelia** curtsies and sits primly, tense; the **Maid** scampers into the background, and adopts a grotesquely submissive pose, as is her custom when she is not required or wishes to be invisible.*

I love you, I love you, I love you, I love you! There.

Now - what do I *mean*? How do I feel when I say that? But first – do I mean need-love or gift-love? Mere selfishness, or saintly, charity? Affection, friendship or Eros? Storge, Philia or Amicitia? Or – just pleasure? *But –* appreciative-pleasure or need-pleasure? And if Eros, in what aspect? Cherub or demon? Eros – or merely Venus?

A test: I shall imagine an exotic Eastern beauty – decked in gold, in silver, ebony locks cascading to the floor – shimmering, expectant, heady with perfume – she looks at me, shyly – she is, say 14 - her lips part, she speaks – in French – ahh! – the silk slips from her fine hips ... Now, how do I *feel!*

Or perhaps something ... short and round; long blond hair; great big ... (*To **Ophelia***) Can I still say I love you? And be honest? When I adore my own creations so? Is this the temptation of the devil? Or God working in mysterious ways?

When I think of you, when I look at you (*He grabs her face*) do I get the required rush of amphetamines? Is phenylethylamine present? Dopamine? Norepinephrine? Do I get a *hit?* Sufficient to prove the presence of True Love? Or just a gentle swell of endorphins?

Ah look at you, you sweet little lovely blushing creature. Blushing – now that's interesting. Do you know why you blush when I speak of love?

Ophelia   (*Overwhelmed*) No my lord.

Hamlet   Hormones, cycles of blood, reproductive turmoil! You are flushed with your female destiny – you are elated, euphoric – yes, you are clearly in love ... (*Fondles her roughly; she jumps; he laughs*) I can play you like a flute!

Ophelia   My lord!

Hamlet   You little tease! The lady doth protest too much methinks.

Ophelia   My lord I *never* tease!

Hamlet   O yes you do – BUT, yes, maybe you don't know it. Feminine wiles; behaviour as instinctive as a cat's with a bird ...

Ophelia   I assure you, my lord -

Hamlet   And is the only way to get you out of black to put you in a wedding gown?

Ophelia   (*Abashed delighted*) My lord?

Hamlet   (*Laughing*) Well?

Ophelia   I hope to marry one day, my lord.

Hamlet   And to what manner of man?

Ophelia A kind man; honest, loving, reliable, faithful ...

Hamlet Oh my dear, you have much to learn about men.

Ophelia Yes?

Hamlet We are driven creatures, Ophelia. Burning with overwhelming desires, tortured with deep longings – our life a passionate mission – a mystical quest for wisdom, for perfection. Whatever and whoever we encounter on this strenuous journey who can help us on our way to God and glory, we must be free to follow.

Ophelia I wonder why men marry at all, my lord, if they require so much freedom.

Hamlet Ah. Some men are lucky enough to find women to marry who understand their needs and responsibilities – who love, support and nurture them, come what may – and are you such a one?

Ophelia Well – I think ...

Hamlet Such women are saints! They fly straight to God's bosom when they die!

Ophelia They do?

Hamlet St. Bernard of Clairvaux, sermon 88.

Ophelia You are very learned, my lord!

Hamlet And I can see you are hungry for everything I can teach you. (*Handling her*) Your nose isn't exactly as I like it. And I prefer a fuller bottom lip, with a curve like so – good profile, though. Hair with more curl, perhaps? (*To **Maid***) Can that be done?

Oh my little black virgin, my temptress ... (*He turns away suddenly, dismayed and desperate*) O 'tis Satan makes men adore women! I must be strong! Let your thoughts fly heavenward, Hamlet; be not distracted from your purpose. I must go, madam! (*Starts to rush out*)

Ah, here, another! (*Gives her a love letter*) The sonnet is an exacting discipline. Oh that I could I find out the woman's part in me! For there's no motion that tends to vice in man, but I affirm it is the woman's part – all faults that may be named, that hell knows ... (*Leaves distractedly*)

> **Ophelia** *flops down; confused, delighted puzzled, shaken*

Maid Well! I don't know what they teach them at that university ...

Ophelia   Enough. (*She reads the sonnet*) For a start, the meaning of words like 'impediment'? What's 'impediment'? 'Love is not love ... if this be error ... no man ever loved.' (*Pleased; flattered; then confused*) O dear!

Why did he rush off? What did I do wrong? He said my face wasn't right, my hair wasn't right – what makes it right? How do I get it right? Keep it right? What does he *want*? (*She inspects her face in a mirror*)

Maid   Give nothing madam.
Weigh what loss your *honour* may sustain
if with too credent ear you listen to his songs;
or lose your heart, or your chaste treasure open ...
fear it madam, fear it, dear Ophelia ...
Beware canker! Beware contagious blastments!

Ophelia   He's right! What am I but a mass of mindless responses and rushing feelings – a skinful of simmering hormones? And I'm ignorant, uninformed, undisciplined, selfish, lustful, stupid ... Oh WHY do I behave like that? I giggle, I blush; he touches me - I throb, I glow; but is this love? Do I love him? Well what *else* can it be?

Does he love me?

He says I tease him. *Do* I? If he *feels* teased, I must! Oh I can't bear it – how could I *do* that? I'm excited when he comes – but I get so confused I can't wait till he leaves – and then I end up like this!

Every time I *swear* I won't behave like that and every time I *do*! Why am I so *weak*? Why am I so stupid?

> *She looks at* **Virgin Mary**, *wherever she has been established.*

O Mary, mother of us, how do I find out what I'm supposed to want?

Maid   Be wary madam, best safety lies in *fear* ...

> *Polonius enters unobserved during the following.*

Ophelia   Oh I'm so sick of this! Pack my bags girl, I'm going to travel the world. Carthage, Alexandria, Pompeii, Jerusalem, Babylon, Lesbos, Atlantis ... Terra Incognita ...

Polonius   (*Laughing*) Except you will be raped, cooked and eaten at your first port of call. Foolish girl.

> *He thrusts a pile of coloured clothes at her.*

Tis sweet and commendable in your nature, Ophelia,
To give these mourning duties to your mother

But you must know, your mother lost a mother,
that mother lost hers, qua qua qua qua ...
But to persevere
in obstinate condolement is a course of
impious stubbornness; tis unwomanly grief;
it shows a will most incorrect to heaven,
a heart unfortified, a mind impatient,
an understanding simple and unschooled;
fie, tis a fault to heaven, a fault to nature,
to reason most absurd, whose common theme is death of mothers.

Ophelia   Aye sir, it is common.

Polonius   I charge you now to take that black stuff *off*! The Queen herself
has sent me with these gowns and begs you please to choose one. Child, this
is a *wedding*. You can't wear black to the Queen's wedding!

Ophelia   I have that within which passes show, these but the trappings and
the suits of woe.

Polonius   I'm not concerned with the woe inside, as long as there are a few
trappings of jollity *outside*. So look to it!

>   *Polonius leaves taking the **Maid**, who is submissive.*

Ophelia   (*Throws clothes down.*)
O that this too too solid flesh would melt,
Thaw and resolve itself into a dew.
Or that the everlasting had not fixed
His canon 'against self-slaughter. O God! God!
How weary, stale, flat and unprofitable
seem to me all the uses of this world!
Fie on't. Ah fie! Tis an unweeded garden
that grows to seed: things rank and gross in nature possess it merely.

>   *Dusk begins falling.*

That it should come to this.
My mother, two years dead. Nay, not so much, not two.
So excellent a mother, so loving to my father
that she might not beteem the winds of heaven
visit his face too roughly. Heaven on earth
must I remember? Why, she would hang on him
as if increase of appetite had grown
by what it fed on. And yet, within a *month* –
let me not think on it. Frailty thy name is man!
A little month! Before those shoes were old

with which he followed my poor mother's body
Like Bob Hawke, (*or any other recent crying male. If one doesn't come to
mind, Niobe will do*) all tears – why he, even he –
O god, a beast that wants discourse of reason
would have mourned longer – dallied with my maid!
And with the washerwoman, the wet nurse,
the scullery maid, the seamstress, the goatgirl, the milkmaid ...
O most wicked speed, to post
with such dexterity to promiscuous sheets!

> *She is sobbing; she notices the Maid's phial of potion she threw down
> earlier; she picks it up, and looks towards* **Mary**

I should go to church
and there, gazing upon our blessed Virgin
tip the pagan love-child's potion down my gullet –
and fall in love –
never more to doubt my path, my purpose.
Now there's a consummation devoutly to be wished ...

> *Crying, she curls up on the bed. It is now very dark. The* **Maid**
> *comes back bedraggled from her assault, pulling her skirt down.
> Faint yells of fright begin to be audible in the distance. She notices*
> **Ophelia** *and covers her with a blanket, smoothes her hair, devoted.*

Maid   Goodnight Madam.

> *She puts on her hat and coat, gets shopping bags, as the distant
> screams become louder. She stops and listens. Suddenly* **Horatio**
> *and* **Hamlet** *run across the stage yelling, and exit, terrified. A ghost
> in armour (***St Joan***) follows and then gives up, panting, centre
> stage. The* **Maid** *is paralysed with fear.*

St Joan   (*Yelling after them*) Non, non, you've missed the point! Where
did everybody go? Oh merde! Listen, listen; for goodness' sake *listen!*

> *The* **Maid**, *stunned, crosses herself, and falls to her knees, praying.*

Why will men never listen! Why do they hear only what they *want* to hear?
They've got it all wrong. Merde! I'll have to come back tomorrow night and
try *again!*

> *She sees the* **Maid**.

Ah! Mademoiselle! Mark me. (*She refers to her notes, and adopts as ghostly
a voice as she can manage*)

My hour is almost come when I to sulph'rous and tormenting flames must
render up myself – (*she rolls her eyes*) - again!

I could a tale unfold whose lightest word
would harrow up thy soul, freeze thy young blood,
make thy two eyes, like stars, start from their spheres,
thy knotted and combined locks to part
and each particular hair to stand on end ...

> *The **Maid**, already in this condition, screams and runs.*

No! Mademoiselle, please. Come back! Oh 'orrible, 'orrible, most 'orrible ...

> *St **Joan** slopes off, fed up at not being able to get anyone's
> attention.*

> *It is now completely dark. There are a few night noises (preferably
> provided by live actors); a Morepork; ghosts; earthquake
> rumbles ...*

Scene 2

*... which quickly become morning noises; rooster, birds; and a quick
dawn.*

Ophelia *is aside with her diary and a book, reading; unaware of
Hamlet and **Horatio** who enter; **Hamlet** with thesaurus, bored;
and **Horatio** with pen and paper, inspired.*

Hamlet   *(Reading from thesaurus)* ... sublime, heavenly, superb, glorious,
ravishing, gorgeous, highly coloured; beaming, sparkling, magnificent,
curvaceous ... well stacked ...

Horatio   Why not just – 'lovely'?

Hamlet   Lovely. Love. *(Looking it up)* No score.

Horatio   No score?

Hamlet   Tennis. Hmm. Desire, affection ... uxoriousness ...

Horatio   What's wrong with 'thou art more lovely' – it's simple, direct –

Hamlet   Simple; yes, she has trouble with big words. Then what?

Horatio   ... 'and more' something else ...

Hamlet   Something else. *(He thinks, frustrated)* Oh for a muse of fire that
would ascend the brightest heaven of invention! Umm – sexy, shapely ...

Horatio   More shapely than summer?

Hamlet   Well what then?

Horatio   Umm ... gentle, sweet, warm ...

Hamlet   Luscious, tempting ...

Horatio   Temperate! Yes, temperate! Yes, you see because then you can go on about what's *wrong* with the weather ... (*He scribbles excitedly*)

Hamlet   What's *wrong* with it? Strange approach for a love poem. Still, if it keeps her wondering, that's good. Keep her sweet. Keep her onside. Keep her on her toes.

Horatio   There! (*He shows it to* **Hamlet**)

Hamlet   (*He reads it*) ... did you have to bring death into it?

Horatio   But we need the final couplet still ...

Hamlet   Something about love, please!

> *They wander aside, as* **Polonius** *enters with books, bumping into* **Hamlet** *and bowing in cringing apology.*

Hamlet   These tedious old fools.

> **Hamlet** *and* **Horatio** *wander off, and* **Polonius** *charges up to* **Ophelia**.

Polonius   (*Bellowing*) Good God, Ophelia, cast thy nighted colour OFF I say!

> *He plucks at her dress –* **Ophelia** *starts to rip her clothes off in a panic. The* **Maid** *rushes on with shopping, hurriedly takes off her hat and coat revealing garlic and a rabbit's foot pinned to her raggy frock.*

Polonius   You're late, girl!

Maid   Beg pardon sir, we have sickness ...

Polonius   Stop gabbling and help her get that thing off!

> *The* **Maid** *helps* **Ophelia** *undress, till she stands there miserably in limp singlet and bloomers.*

Right. And now, something touching the Lord Hamlet.
Tis told me he hath very oft of late
given private time to you; and you yourself

have of your audience been most free and bounteous.
What is between you? Give me up the truth.

Ophelia He hath my lord, of late made many tenders of his affection for me.

Polonius Affection! Pooh! You speak like a green girl
unsuited in such perilous circumstances.
Do you believe his tenders, as you call them?

Ophelia ... I do not know, my lord, what I should think ...

Polonius Marry, I will teach you: think yourself a baby
that you have taken these tenders for true pay
which are not sterling. Tender yourself more dearly;
or – not to crack the wind of a poor phrase,
running it thus – you'll tender me a fool.
Your chastity's the jewel of our house, bequeathed down from many
illustrious ancestors.

Ophelia Yes my lord.

Polonius Lord Hamlet is a prince out of thy star; this must not be.
In short –
I would not, in plain terms, from this time forth
have you so slander any moment's leisure
as to give words or talk to the Lord Hamlet.
Is that quite clear?

Ophelia Quite clear, my lord.

Polonius And now – you have finished sorting my notes?

> The **Maid** thrusts a pile of papers at **Ophelia** who gives them to him.

Good. Now by noon on Friday – here; The Unfinished Works of Puncher and Wattman.

> He thrusts a pile of heavy books into **Ophelia**'s arms.

I require all references to tennis. There will be several. And any mention of skulls; of that possibility I'm less certain. But remember to rest often - women must beware forcing the brain. It leads to nervousness, anaemia, stunted growth, anorexia and flat chests. Your children will be puny and enfeebled. (*He fondles the **Maid***) And remember what I've said regarding Hamlet.

> **Polonius** leaves.

Ophelia (*Heaving the books at the* **Maid**) He shows me the steep and thorny way to heaven, while like a puffed and reckless libertine, himself the primrose path of dalliance treads and recks not his own rede!

Maid He gives good advice, madam. Best safety lies in fear.

The **Maid** *offers one of the coloured frocks, hopefully.*

Ophelia Damn him! (*She knocks it aside and holds out the black dress*)

Maid (*Putting on her black stuff again*) O madam, take care! Do as your father bids you! Remember, remember how bad Prince Hamlet makes you feel!

Ophelia Yes, he does make me feel bad. He makes fun of me.

Maid He upsets you, he takes you for granted ...

Ophelia He assumes I'll be there whenever he wants!

Maid He humiliates you ...

Ophelia Hmm. I wonder. What if I refuse his company, what then?

Maid Oh yes madam! Avoid him, forget him!

Ophelia It will give him a shock! He will have to stop and think. Pull up his socks. He will realise Ophelia is *not* so easily won. O yes! If he wants me, he must woo me!

> **Ophelia** *moves excitedly back to her diary to write down her new resolution, as* **Hamlet** *and* **Horatio** *come back into focus. The* **Maid** *quietly tidies up and leaves meanwhile.*

Horatio (*Who has found the final couplet*)
'So long as men can breathe, or eyes can see
So long lives this, and this gives life to thee.'

Hamlet Terrific! Who cares what it means, it rhymes! (*Throwing the thesaurus down*) Oh, Horatio. Why are we in bondage to these creatures?

Horatio Bondage?

Hamlet It's so undignified. I mean – what a piece of work is a man. How noble in reason, how infinite in faculties, in form and moving; how express and admirable in action, how like an angel in apprehension; how like a god! The beauty of the world! The paragon of animals! And yet – a mere woman can have our hearts in chains with one flash of her evil eyes.

Horatio We are Adam's sons; still easily tempted.

Hamlet   It flies in the face of nature that creatures so base should have such power over us.

Horatio   Yet Christ was born of woman ...

Hamlet   But what a woman! You can't compare real women with her! And anyway – a virgin birth is – *clean.*

Horatio   Are they base, or just different, my lord? They have a very different function.

Hamlet   Just 'different'? Heresy, Horatio. The prof. would turn purple if he heard you. 'A female is a female by virtue of her *lack* of qualities' – Aristotle. 'A female is a defective male' – Thomas Aquinas.

Horation   Whatever they may lack, they do have a rather striking *extra* ability ...

Hamlet   Sprogging? Oh, Horatio – but that function is *all.* They are womb-driven. They have no *choice,* they *must sprog* - and so – fight for a man, fight off other women, trap a man, keep a man, fight for domestic power, keep the man in chains. And we cannot blame them! They are slaves to their animal instinct; every organ is geared, is focused, for the achievement of these ends. The dominant organ is not brain, but womb. We are basically dealing with a creature closer to animals than men. Men's inability to sprog – thank God – is what assures his special aptitude for everything else!

Horatio   I've known a few men pretty focused on an organ other than the brain ...

Hamlet   There are a few rare women with higher abilities, to be fair. Such women are aware of their sex's greater responsibility to acquire purity of body and soul, to do penance for the sins of Eve ...

Horatio   And such women surpass us, my lord. The female sex may be cursed by the potential for a greater depth of evil; but by the same token, conquering that flaw requires greater moral strength; is worthy of greater praise than anything we can do who are not so sorely tested.

Hamlet   Surpass us! O heresy, Horatio. Such women are rare, such women are saints – but still *women*. But anyway I'm talking about the rest of them – your run-of-the-mill woman – I mean take my *mother,* for example ...

*They come across **Ophelia**, reading her book.*

Horatio   And because female saints are rare, we should count ourselves truly blessed when we find one in our midst.

***Horatio**, as ever very tense and formal in **Ophelia**'s presence,* *tortured by a mix of feelings which shall be revealed anon, bows very properly to her. She glances suspiciously; then is alarmed to see* **Hamlet** *there.*

Hamlet   Ah, how now Ophelia! *(He takes her book, and laughs)* Romance! What did I tell you Horatio! *(He gives book to* **Horatio***)* Here she is, the little poppet, in full mourning, absorbed in erotic trivia. 'Love in the Time of the Plague'.

Ophelia   Horatio. Please inform the Lord Hamlet that I am not ashamed of my desire to understand love. God is love. Therefore if I understand love, I come closer to God.

Hamlet   A touching attempt at logic, my sweet; and I have heard many whores use the same argument.

Ophelia   My lord!

> **Hamlet** *snatches her diary; she struggles to retain it, horrified. He reads out mockingly:*

Hamlet   'How can I be sure of his love? How can I show mine honourably?' (*He tosses it to* **Horatio***, laughing.)*

Ophelia   Please also inform him that I have been instructed by my father neither to speak nor meet with him again.

Hamlet   'Please inform!' What new game is this!? Not meet? Then we shall have to meet in secret, far away from prying eyes. (*He holds her face; she breaks away; he grabs her wrist*)

Ophelia   Please inform the Lord Hamlet that I have no desire to speak with him or meet with him in secret, or in any other way ...

Hamlet   What?!

> **Horatio** *pushes the poem they have just finished into* **Hamlet***'s hand.*

Hamlet   What's this?

Horatio   A work of romance, my lord.

Hamlet   Aha! Here, my little tease; can you refuse the outpourings of my soul?

Ophelia   *(She nearly can't; but resists)* Please inform my Lord Hamlet that I am also forbidden to receive any letters from him. (*She turns to go.*)

Hamlet   Stay where you are madam!

Ophelia stops; Hamlet tears the sonnet up slowly, and drops it.

I am delighted to see that you obey others besides your father. Interfering fool! (*He grabs her wrist again; it hurts her*) I am most gratified that you consider some courtesies still due to your future king. Oh, I am honoured, madam.

He bows mockingly, as Laertes enters

Laertes   My lords, the King requests your presence.

Hamlet   O he does, does he?

Laertes   My lord, unhand my sister – you know the rules.

Laertes grabs her other wrist; they yank her back and forth.

Hamlet   We all know the rules Laertes, otherwise there'd be no fun in breaking them, now would there?

Laertes   Oh I agree; but the amount of fun depends on the number of brothers you have to deal with later, whose honour depends on the behaviour of their sisters.

Ophelia   (*To Laertes, under breath*) Piss off!

Hamlet   Laertes, thou art as dear to me as any brother. How could Hamlet wrong Laertes?

Laertes   My sister's virginity is of great concern to me, my lord.

Hamlet   Ah, would that it were *my* concern!

They laugh, and drop Ophelia.

Ah, men! (*He puts his arms round them*) The company of men! Out of the sickly air and into a fresh, wholesome breeze! Oh I would grapple thee to me with hoops of steel. Straightforward, honest, brave, healthy men!

He gives Horatio a big kiss – he is surprised, confused. Ophelia is upset, embarrassed. The Maid enters.

Maid   Madam ...

Hamlet   O father spare me. Another damned woman!

Laertes   Ah, but this is a lively one . .

They both grab the Maid, laughing.

Hamlet   Ah now, look. Ophelia. *That's* what I call a breast –

Laertes   (*Lifting the* **Maid***'s skirt*) Legs! Howzat!

Hamlet   That's more like it; and what about her rump (*Revealing it*) Ah yes, this is *my* type of girl ...

> *The* **Maid** *struggles to deliver her message.*

Maid   Madam, the Queen requests your presence –

Horatio   And do not forget my lord that *we* must see the King.

Hamlet   Ah the King, the King. Here, Horatio. (*He pushes the* **Maid** *into his arms*) I have urgent business.

> **Horatio** *is horrified and pushes the* **Maid** *to* **Laertes,** *who grabs her.* **Hamlet** *and* **Laertes** *laugh.)*

Why, that's the longest relationship you've ever had with a woman, I do believe, Horatio!

Laertes   Wise man! (*Bows*) My lords; sister.

> *He leaves with the* **Maid***, and scuffling is heard off.*

Hamlet   The King awaits. Please beg this creature to excuse us, Horatio, as I'm not permitted to speak to it directly. Come.

> **Hamlet** *goes;* **Horatio** *follows but then turns back, picks up* **Ophelia***'s book and diary and gives them to her, formally. She glares at him.*

Ophelia   Oh *very* kind.

> *There is a tense moment between them, and* **Horatio** *leaves.* **Ophelia** *stands silent, angry, dejected.*

Shit. O shit shit shit. He doesn't give a shit.

> *She picks up the pieces of sonnet and tries to put them together – the bits she can read move her – she is confused again. The* **Maid** *enters, bedraggled again, rearranging her clothes. Pause, as* **Ophelia** *looks the* **Maid** *over; and then checks out her body, lifting her skirt etc. comparing legs, breast, 'rump' with her own. She finishes, and stands dejected.*

Maid   The Queen, madam, awaits you.

> **Ophelia** *moves to the Queen's area, followed by the* **Maid** *as the* **Queen** *enters.*

Scene 3

Queen   My, look how you've grown! *(Ophelia curtsies)* Oh, I have been remiss! Two years with no mother to advise and direct you ... Off with it!

The Maid removes Ophelia's black clothes.

My darling girl, you cannot wear black to my wedding – you cannot wear black ever again, you pretty thing!

Ophelia   The prince wears black, madam ...

Queen   Oh sweetie, he's a man; they can do what they like; and he only does it to get attention, you know what men are like. Best to ignore him. But *you* – a girl must make the best of herself; display her wares ...

Ophelia   Wares?

Queen   *(To Maid)* Start please. *(And back to Ophelia)* You wait, when we've finished you'll dazzle them all.

The Maid starts taking Ophelia's measurements and noting them on a large chart.

Ophelia   But I'm not sure I want to ...

Queen   Not want to dazzle my son?

Ophelia   I ... don't want to attract any attention ...

Queen   My dear child, any girl who doesn't wear foundations attracts a great deal of attention – of quite the wrong kind! *(Ophelia looks puzzled)* Wobbles, darling. We wobble. It's like a red rag to a bull! Now let's see – good breasts; good legs; good waist; not bad hips ...

Under the Queen's watchful eye the Maid starts a fantastical cosmetic and corset fitting process; e.g. eyebrow plucking, leg waxing, arm oiling, nails, garish face mask, fierce corsetry, grossly padded bra, chastity belt, miles of bandage wound tightly around her etc. which continues throughout the following, slowly immobilising her.

Ophelia   'Good' I want to be 'good'. But what do they mean by 'good'? Healthy? Strong? Fashionably shaped? What's a 'bad' leg? An immoral leg? A naughty leg? A leg that won't go to heaven? Good and bad! What do they mean?

Queen Now then, why so anxious?

Ophelia I don't want to wobble!

Queen And neither you will. You will delight – but not over-excite. *This* is the art that you must master.

Ophelia Why?

Queen Why?

Ophelia I don't want to delight OR over-excite ...

Queen Oh. You want to disgust?

Ophelia No! No, I mean ... no, but ...

Queen If the prince discards you, as he will if you don't pull yourself together, what other man will dare touch you? And *then* where will you be? What will you do?

Ophelia Well ... my father ... ?

Queen He's an old man! He will die, your brother will inherit everything; he will marry. What's your position them? Utterly dependant. What will you DO? Who will protect you?

Ophelia From what?

Maid Other men.

Queen As with any job, the boss decides the conditions. They want sweet breath, big tits, endless sex, terrific food, emotional support – then do it. They want a coper, cope. They want a helpless airhead, do it. They want kids, do it. They don't? Hmm; well come to me and I'll help you out when the time comes. *(To the Maid)* That reminds me, I hear there is a new ... cure?

Maid Yes ma'am – a mixture of horseflies, leeches, turnips, monkey brains and mercury. Very effective.

Queen Good, I'll place an order. And one thing they all want, one vision that's in all their heads, whatever they tell you – a pure, sweet, submissive little virgin. A *virgin* mind. So watch it. No wobbling.

Ophelia Can't I just be myself? ...

Queen 'Be yourself'? Ha! Only men have that luxury – and you don't want to be like a man, do you? Men can be themselves – but we have to *work* at being women ...

Ophelia What? Work at it?

Queen   Yes, yes! You see, my dear - men are at the centre of the world. They don't have to define themselves. They can take their masculinity for granted, whereas we ... I know, it's tough, but it's our duty.

And think of the poor dears, sweating away in boardroom and on battlefield – for *us* – our protection and support; our children. We're at their mercy, for sure; but in return we have it easy. Men have their needs, their fantasies – it's our job to divine them and provide them. Let's bring a little sweetness and joy into their dour little lives – we're shaped this way to please them, after all – so what's a few ribbons, a bit of paint? For the satisfaction of being the inspirers of male glory ...

Ophelia   Our shape? It thought it was ... for children ... ?

Queen   Don't look so glum. Of course it's all tiresome at times, but we learn to get our own way; I can show you how to handle them – but cleverly, so they don't know! You can manipulate him, you can fool him – the hen can rule the roost and the cock thinks *he* does ...!

Ophelia   They can't *all* be fools!

Queen   Children! They're all children! The darlings, they never grow up.

Ophelia   But when I marry I want an adult, not a child! I want a friend, a ... a partner! A husband I can be honest with!

Queen   Honest? Ha! Only equals can be friends and partners. Men and women are not equals. You can't be 'friends' with a man!

Ophelia   I DON'T BELIEVE IT!

>   *She tries to struggle but is too constrained by now; the **Maid** calms her.*

Queen   Ophelia! For your poor dear mother's sake, listen to me. IF you want happiness, security, children, comfort, all the things she would want for you, then listen. Imagine if she were here now, right in front of you ...

Ophelia   NO!

Queen   My dear, you must listen to me!

Ophelia   NO!! NO!!

Queen   Oh, *children!* (*She bursts into tears*) If you only knew how we suffered for you, then you'd listen ... One day ... you'll see ... just you wait ...!

Ophelia   Your majesty, I'm sorry. I don't mean to sound ungrateful (*Still the **Queen** sobs*) Oh dear! Of course I want happiness, security ... Oh Ma'am I'm so sorry! And children, of course I want children!

*During the following speech the **Maid** applies something –
cucumber slices? – to **Ophelia's** eyes as a finishing touch; so by the
end she is not only immobile, but blind.*)

Queen *(Recovering somewhat)* Oh, children, children, children. Why do
we do it? Hours and hours of intense pain, for our sins. And then – your
body splits in two – and out comes – another person. It's absolutely absurd.
Absurd and horrifying. Knowing that your body – *your* body, that you
thought you *knew* – can just split open and splurt out a whole new person;
just like that. Ludicrous.

And it throws you; it's thoroughly bewildering. You are completely tossed
out of yourself, you can never be absolutely certain of anything ever again...
That's why men don't like knowing about it; it rattles their little certainties.
They like to think we take it in our stride, find it all 'natural', you know.
When in fact the process is as extraordinary and frightening for us as it
would be for them – if it happened to them. You, girl – you've had children.
Don't you agree?

Maid O yes, yes your majesty. Your body is shattered, then your sleep is
shattered.

Queen All the tidy little structures you've built up around you – for
your emotional survival, your protection – collapse like a pack of cards ...
everything you believed is thrown into question ...

Maid You thought you knew what love meant ...

Queen Ah, and then you look in the ugly little face of this child you've
made and you know the word 'love' wasn't coined till the first mother looked
at the first baby.

Maid We do stupid things for men sometimes but it's only for our children
we'll do ...

Maid & Queen   ... absolutely anything.

Queen Absolutely anything. But don't let men know this. They get jealous.
They like to think *they* invented love.

Maid It is a strange god who feels he punished Eve by giving her
childbirth; the gateway to the greatest love we can know. How can such a gift
be called punishment?

Queen Shsh! Enough, girl! The walls have ears.

Maid But be wary – they worship Mother & Child – but they despise
women and babies!

Queen Enough! Back to work! And above all, Ophelia, make sure you have sons ...

Ophelia Sons?

Queen Just keep going till you have one. A woman with a son is powerful.

Ophelia And I'm a daughter.

Queen Exactly. You're only a daughter. Next is wife, and then mother of sons. And if you play your cards right, the wife of a prince, then a queen; and then a mother of kings. What you look like at my wedding today could decide your future.

Ophelia Ah. I see.

Pause.

Queen My dear, you must understand that men are not intentionally cruel, or vicious, or devious, or inconsiderate. It's just that self-interest is woven into the very fabric of their being; their natural birthright is to have things their own way. They feel they have a right not to suffer, and not to care who hurts. So you see, it's not intentional. You mustn't take it personally. It's just the way they are! Ah, where would the world be without its adorable angry young men? And now I must rest. A word of advice ...

Ophelia Yes?

Queen Don't *think* too much my dear. You'll get wrinkles.

*The **Queen** leaves. **Ophelia** is immobilised by her corsetry and masks. Pause.*

Ophelia Is there life before death?

*Pause. She slowly feels the mask on her face, the stuff in her hair; then the corsets etc.; and suddenly panics, leaps up and starts ripping it all off, yelling. During the frenzy the **Maid** helps, anguished. Finally it's done and **Ophelia** stands dishevelled in her underwear again, wild and panting; the **Maid** moaning quietly aside.*

How come I turned into a woman!!? Can't I just stay a person? I didn't want to be a woman; *or* a man. I didn't ask to be either. It just happened. I just want to be a *person!*

People carry on as if I made a choice; as if I must be pleased; as if I saw what a woman's life was like and said 'Yes, I'll have that I think', like choosing fish in a market; as if I made a deliberate choice I now have to be responsible for;

if I don't make a good fist of it then I'm to blame. 'I made my bed; now I must lie in it'. But I *didn't* make the bed! I *won't* bloody lie in it!

(Feeling her body thoughtfully.) I didn't ask for any of this – it just *grew*. I don't know what I'm supposed to *do* with it. All these knobs and blobs and hairy bits; bleeding bits, for heaven's sake! What is it all? How did I become this mobile tub of female sexual parts? How did *I* get in *here*?

Pinch me. *(The **Maid** does so.)* Bite me. *(She does so.)* What is all this? Why is it me? *Is* it me? Why aren't *you* me?

Maid   Madam, you're overtired; you should sleep, you should pray ...

Ophelia   DAMN prayer! Damn mothers, damn children, damn kings and queens and virgins – *damn* virgins! *(She addresses **Mary**)* Especially you, you sinless wonder! You sexless mutant! One look at you and I know I've failed; every day, every minute! We try so hard to be like you - how about *you* trying to be like *us* for a change! Give being a *real* woman a go! Try being a virgin and a mother down here, and see how good *you* are at it! *You* try period pain!

Maid   *(On her knees, distressed, praying)* Oh madam! You will be punished! You will be hung by the tongue from a burning tree!

Ophelia   Well, she's got an unfair advantage! Born without sin – of *course* purity's a breeze! I turn into a woman without my consent, and then I'm expected to be like *her*! Is that fair! What psychotic clown set *these* rules?

> *Hamlet strides in, with a feeble bunch of flowers.*

Hamlet   Madam, my wretched mother has informed me that you have come to your senses, and has instructed me to escort you to this damned nuptial.

Ophelia   And my wretched father has instructed me to have nothing further to do with *you*!

Hamlet   *(Shocked at **Ophelia's** appearance and cheek)* Aagh! So – you still obey him before your Queen, and future King?

Ophelia   YES!

Hamlet   *(Throwing down the flowers)* You're going to regret this! Who the hell do you think you are??

> *Hamlet storms off. **Ophelia** is at first triumphant, then horrified as she realises the extent of her blasphemy and insubordination. She picks up the flowers.*

Ophelia Oh no, what have I done! Oh, forgive me, forgive me! Oh I didn't mean … Oh, blessed Virgin! Oh God! Look, he brought me flowers! Oh what am I to do? What am I to do??

Maid Madam please … (*Weeping, holding up one of **Polonius'** coloured frocks*) Please!

Ophelia Oh no! Do I *have* to go?

Maid Oh ma'am, if you don't you risk great danger …

Ophelia Danger?

Maid The times are strange. Ghosts are afoot; crop circles are appearing in the barley fields! We must be careful of our feelings, watch our tongues lest we invite these evil forces and powers into our lives …

*She lets the **Maid** put on the frock, wipe the mask off her face etc.*

Ophelia I was happy when I was a little girl, you know.

Maid You're a woman now. The rules have changed.

Ophelia I want to *stay* a little girl. I don't want to grow up – I will *not* grow up. How do I flatten out these?

Maid Ma'am, everyone will laugh at you!

Ophelia No way out then. Ridicule whichever way I turn.

There is a knock at the door

He's back! Quick, my hair – the flowers. (*Rush to finish tidying her.*) Come in.

***Horatio** enters nervously, with a healthy bunch of flowers.*

Horatio Madam, it is the Queen's wish that I accompany you to the wedding celebrations.

Ophelia *You?*

Horatio Yes madam.

Ophelia What have you done to deserve such punishment?

Horatio Her majesty is aware of your father's request and approves of your obedience …

Ophelia But Hamlet has no partner now. It would be rather more fitting for you to escort *him*, wouldn't it?

Horatio   *(Very embarrassed)* I'm sure *he* would not agree.

Ophelia   And now I'm forced on you, poor man. Oh poor, poor Horatio. He hurts you just as much as hurts me, doesn't he? I shouldn't be so unkind. Oh what a sorry pair of rivals we are ...

> *She flops down and starts to cry;* **Horatio** *is mortified and awkwardly tries to find consoling words.*

Horatio   Now, now Ophelia – madam – you have no cause to cry! Hamlet loves *you*; of this I'm sure. When you appear tonight, your father, the Queen, the whole court will be delighted at your transformation. Um. I will ensure that you have time with the prince to speak, and solve your differences. All will be well.

> *Still she cries.* **Horatio** *is distressed.*

Horatio   Ophelia, madam; please ...!

> **Ophelia** *pulls herself together.*

Ophelia   Horatio – I have of late - but wherefore I know not - lost all my mirth. This goodly frame, the earth, seems to me a sterile promontory; this most excellent canopy the air, look you, this brave o'er hanging firmament, this majestical roof fretted with golden fire – why it appeareth no other thing to me than a foul and pestilent congregation of vapours.

What a piece of work is a woman, Horatio. What gifts, what powers, what joys await me! But I assure you, my womanhood delights me as little as it delights you!

Horatio   Ma'am, your womanhood delights *Hamlet*. Be patient with his moods. Let his love into your heart, and you will find joy again!

Ophelia   Horatio, how loyal you are to him! What greater love is there than this!

> *Wedding music can be faintly heard.*

What a sad and silly pair we are. *(Smiles, and takes his flowers)* Well, come on then! Nothing ventured, nothing gained!

Horatio   Bravo! There is much to look forward to ma'am – a whole week of festivities – musicians, feasts, theatre, magic, morris dancing ...

> *The* **Maid** *gets up, delighted, and wipes* **Ophelia's** *face etc.*

Ophelia   You're right, Horatio. I am determined to enjoy myself. *(She offers her arm)* Best foot forward!

Horatio   Oh, ma'am! Bravo!

*They leave cheerfully enough. The **Maid,** relieved, tidies up the mess as the lights dim and the noises of celebration increase. A crowd of wedding partygoers dance around the stage with sparklers, hooters, balloons – including **St Joan,** who is still trying to get someone's attention. As the **Maid** gathers her bags to go home, **St Joan** spies her and accosts her.*

St Joan   Mademoiselle, please listen!

*This time the terrified **Maid** is ready for her, and chants and waves garlic and crosses at her, as if she were a vampire. Meanwhile the ghost of **Ophelia's mother** also enters, carrying a rose, posing palms up, head inclined, by **Ophelia's** bed. **St Joan** gives up on the **Maid,** who runs off, shrieking, as the partygoers leave and the music subsides.*

St Joan   Why will no one ever listen?

***Ophelia** rushes on distressed, confetti covered; **St Joan** accosts her.*

St Joan   Ah! Excusez-moi! I have message ...

Ophelia   (*Interrupting*) Did you hear that? Did you hear what that drunken oaf said to me?

St Joan   Eh? Drunken what?

Ophelia   Hamlet, of course, Prince Hamlet! Why does he say such things? Why is he punishing me?

*She wails; **St Joan** gives up in despair and leaves, muttering French expletives. **Ophelia** turns and sees her **mother's** ghost. She thinks it's a vision of **Mary** – she crosses herself, and faints onto the bed.*

Holy Mary Mother of God!

Mother   (*Gabbling sweetly*) It's your mother darling, just your mother, sorry I gave you such a fright. But you're so upset I just had to come to let you know that this is the worst bit – it doesn't get worse than this. It's a struggle to get to that wedding day but once it's over darling, everything changes. All you have to do is play house and dress up, and dream, pick flowers and play with your babies, and tell the servants what to do occasionally – there's no need for any more growing up! You can go back to being ten years old if you like and stay there for the rest of your life! What fun! There now - don't you feel better?

And they like that, they like you being a little girl; just don't talk too much dear; just smile and be polite, he'll think you're the cleverest thing – act shy, a bit scared, blush when he touches you, they like that; make *him* happy and you're happy, it's a funny thing; forget self, men and children first; sacrifice, rewards will come...

During the following she slowly fades and backs out, throwing the rose onto the bed before she leaves. The light starts dimming.

And darling – don't *think* too much, just smile, he'll think you're the sweetest thing ... and darling – don't trust other women – women are treacherous, sly, scheming, deceitful ... don't think, smile, wait, forget self ... patience, don't think, don't talk ... smile ... forget self dear, forget self ...

> **Ophelia** *groans, as if having a nightmare. Night falls, to the usual night sounds. She sleeps. Pause.*

Scene 4

Morning sounds. **Ophelia** *is still prostrate on the bed, her mother's rose beside her. Three old* **women** *scamper in and gather round her, whispering, nattering. One has a wooden bowl of herbal tonic.*

1   Oh look, she's waking up.

2   Good morning dear.

1   Here you are, drink this, it'll make you feel better ...

Ophelia   What is it?

3   A woman's tonic – shhh, it's a secret.

1   We don't want to be burned as witches.

2   It's more effective if it's drunk at the full moon...

Ophelia   Why?

3   But it will still do you good.

Ophelia   What's it for?

> *The* **Maid** *enters; coat, hat, bags; she has acquired more tokens and charms about her person. During the following she slowly gets caught up in the atmosphere.*

1   We all saw you at the wedding dear.

3   What a state you were in – what a kerfuffle.

1   We saw your aura.

2   Your moral outrage.

1   We know exactly how you feel.

Ophelia   My moral outrage?

3   Drink it dear.

Ophelia   What's in it?

1   Trust us, trust us, our wisdom is centuries old ...

    Ophelia *drinks; it's revolting. She lies back.*

2   Read the dregs, Hecuba.

1   I see strife, I see gender war; I see the initial X ...

Ophelia   Gender war?

2   The women are stirring in the kingdom, Ophelia ...

3   You know, we all know, that something is rotten in the state!

2   We know what's rotten ...

3   Over and over we tell them; over and over and over, but will they listen?

2   All those men sitting round the council table.

1   We want to be there too to enrich the state with our instinct, our intuition – to bring our wisdom into the light of day.

Ophelia   At council? You want a *vote*?

All Three   (*Fists in the air*) Yes! Shh ... it's the only way!

Ophelia   But – sitting in that musty chamber day after day – with all those dusty, smelly, boring old men – why?

1   They call us irrational – look where male reason has got us!

2   Women are the moral guardians of society!

1   The keepers of sacred hearth and home!

3   The soul of the Family!

2   The moral fibre of the nation!

1   The civilising influence, the purifying stream ...

2   Women are God's police!

3   Without us men are mere savages.

1   And what is the council but a tableful of savages, barbarians who ignore their wives, their mothers and the church ...

2   We all saw them last night; blaspheming, philandering, vomiting, urinating ...

1   We need passion! Zeal! Not rational argument!

2   The state is in chaos; wars threaten, economies weaken ...

3   Strange lights appear in the sky ...

1   Ghosts walk ...

Ophelia   Ghosts? (*She picks up the rose, and half remembers her 'vision'*)

Maid   (*Possessed*)
In the most high and palmy state of Rome
a little ere the mighty Julius fell,
the graves stood tenantless, and the sheeted dead
did squeak and gibber in the Roman streets ...
churchyards yawn, and hell itself breathes out contagion to the world ...

    *The **Maid** collapses in a trance.*

3   Aye – stars with trains of fire ...

1   And dews of blood ...

2   Disasters in the sun ...

All three   Bubble bubble, toil and trouble ...

1   We must be there to civilise.

2   To defend the sanctity of home and family.

3   The nobility of housewife and mother.

1   To ban the demon drink!

All three   BAN THE DEMON DRINK!   Will you join us?

    *Pause. **Ophelia** looks pensive, then vomits noisily back into the* *bowl.*

2   There. Just the *thought* of alcohol makes her sick.

1   Rest dear.

3   We'll come back later when you're feeling stronger.

> *The **women** scamper off, nattering. The **Maid** comes to, takes the bowl and exits. **Ophelia** is alone; she groans, feeling foul. Pause.*

Ophelia   To be or not to be – that is the question;
whether tis nobler in the mind to suffer
the slings and arrows of outrageous fortune
or to take arms against a sea of troubles,
and by opposing, end them. To die, to sleep –
no more; and by a sleep to say we end
the heartache and the thousand natural shocks
that flesh is heir to. Tis a consummation
devoutly to be wished. To die, to sleep;
to sleep;

> *She observes her mother's rose again, and faintly remembers her 'nightmare'*

perchance to dream.
Aye, there's the rub;
for in that sleep of death what dreams may come
when we have shuffled off this mortal coil
must give us pause. There's the respect
that makes calamity of so long life.
For who would put up with the whips, the scorns, the pain,
the pangs, the cramps, the sweats, the spurns, the burdens,
the agonies of life, when you could easily end it all with a sharp fruit knife?
Except for the dread of something after death –
the undiscovered country, from whose bourn
no traveller returns ... it puzzles the will
and makes us rather bear those ills we have
than fly to others that we know not of.

> *The **Maid** quietly returns during the following.*

Thus conscience does make cowards of us all
and thus the native hue of resolution
is sicklied o'er with the pale cast of thought,
and enterprises of great pitch and moment
with this regard, their currents turn awry
and lose the name of *action.*

Maid   Madam, will you pray with me?

Ophelia   My mother. She used to frown when I got excited ... I saw malice in her eyes ...

Maid   Ma'am the time is out of joint –

Ophelia   She will never forgive me for refusing to be like her – and I am ravaged with guilt for having to refuse. Two years of mourning for the lack of love between us ...

Maid   Oh ma'am don't speak that way!

Ophelia   Quiet, let me sleep. I don't feel well.

> ***Hamlet*** *bursts in 'in disarray', in a rage, and out of his mind.The following violence works well with the* ***Maid*** *providing the sound FX (visibly) while the actors skilfully mime. The* ***Maid*** *becomes increasingly distressed.*

Hamlet   You faithless, devious, conniving little bitch – who the hell do you think you are?

Ophelia   My lord, my father says ...

Hamlet   *(He hits her)* Your father! Your father! You try playing your games with me you stupid cow, drab, tart, floozy, cunt, hag, spinster, devil's gateway, fright, frump, midwife, bit of fluff! And you'll get everything you're asking for! You remember what you are – woman; commoner! You push no prince around! You obey no doddering father over me!

Ophelia   But my lord ...

Hamlet   Who do you honour? Who? Who? (*Prodding her*)

Ophelia   You my lord, you ... !

Hamlet   (*He continues to hit, drag, prod.*) You lead me on you wretch, you whore, you witch! You drive me crazy with your games, your taunts, your petty jealousies, your devious little rejections; your flirtings, your paintings, your paddings ...

Ophelia   No!

Hamlet   Quiet! – you women, talk talk talk! Your cheek, your lip! Can't keep your mouth shut for a minute*!* (***Ophelia*** *sobs*) Oh, *why* do women get so EMOTIONAL!

You turn me down; *me*; and whose arm are you on last night? Who do you wear colours for, whisper to, confide in, giggle with, slobber over ...

Ophelia No!

Hamlet *My* man! My best friend! In front of the whole court!

Ophelia But the Queen ...!

Hamlet Everyone knows you're mine!

Ophelia But the Queen, my lord ...

Hamlet The Queen, your father! You'll obey anyone but me! You spit in my face! (*He sobs*) Me! Me! *Me!* Weighed down with grief and care, haunted by demons, apparitions – and now betrayed by you. You!

Ophelia These are but wild and whirling words, my lord; you know Horatio would never ...

Hamlet O yes but you, you viper, would bewitch him with your spells and trickery; like Eve would arouse in him evil and lust ...

Ophelia No my lord ...!

Hamlet Ophelia you are headed for damnation. Look to your soul, look to your sins ...

Ophelia Yes, yes my lord ...!

Hamlet The soul dies in lust, Ophelia; when Eve tempted, death, sex and marriage entered the world ...

Ophelia O God ...

Hamlet Eve sinned, so Christ had to die! *You* deserved death, and God had to be crucified!

Ophelia O help me, help me!

Hamlet Oh I've read all about you! Woman! Woman is all that is vile, corrupt and lowly; her body a tornado of blood, bile, urine, phlegm and mucous and the fluid of digested food: - her womb a cauldron of contagion, pus and poisons ... *(**Ophelia** groans)* And all we see is beauty. We are bewitched! Wise men know well enough what monsters you make of them. You are a witch, Ophelia!

Ophelia *No!*

Hamlet It is Satan makes men adore women! Instead of loving our creator we sinfully turn to them ...

Ophelia O what must I do, what must I do?

Hamlet *Get thee to a nunnery!*

Ophelia Oh yes, yes ... but ... !

Hamlet (*Quietening, possessed*) Redeem yourself; purify your soul with chastity, prayer, hardship – you will only be worthy of my love when ... when ...

Ophelia When I am too pure to love you back?

Hamlet Yes! When you deny your sex, and strive to resemble our saviour, the perfect man ...

Ophelia But ...

Hamlet (*Close to her, touching, urgently whispering*) Virginity is all that separates us from the beasts, Ophelia.

Ophelia Yes, yes ...

Hamlet Virgins don't rot when they die; only they are allowed wings in heaven.

Ophelia O my lord ... (*She swoons into him*)

Hamlet A boy who hasn't seen a woman can handle red-hot iron ...

Ophelia O you're so learned, my lord.

Hamlet Do not be a breeder of sinners, Ophelia ... Only a virgin can catch a unicorn!

Ophelia Not breed? Not even to bring more virgins into the world?

Hamlet The marriage most beloved of god is the chaste one ...

> *They are both becoming somewhat carried away with religious passion ...*

Ophelia Like Joseph and Mary – yes ...

Hamlet (*Leaping away*) Ah, marriage! Marriage does make monsters of us all! I say there will be no more marriages! Keep away from me, keep away! Cast no more spells!

Ophelia No, no ... !

Hamlet Sweetest things turn sourest by their deeds – lilies that fester smell far worse than weeds!

> ***Hamlet*** *rushes out, berserk.* ***Ophelia*** *and the* ***Maid*** *fall to their knees, distraught.* ***Ophelia*** *pleads with* ***Mary.***

Ophelia   Oh help me, help me! Fill me with desire for goodness, humility, obedience ... cleanse me, purify me, strip me of my sins, my viciousness! I will spend my life in prayer, in fasting, in denial of all pleasure! Empty my poisoned brain, disinfect my putrid body; shrink me, purge me, beat me, beat me ... (*to the* **Maid**) Beat me!

> *The **Maid** obeys, distraught, throughout the following (walloping the floor just behind **Ophelia** with a bamboo cane is effective). The following speech is punctuated with gasps of pain, therefore.*

Oh outstanding model of sweetness and light! Only woman victorious over the baseness of femaleness! I have been angry, wilful, unnatural, and unwomanly! I have blasphemed. I have disobeyed, I have been selfish, arrogant, critical – I have – I have *thought too much!* Oh heavens stop me thinking! God forgave Magdalene! Beg him to forgive me! *(to **Maid**)* Useless woman! My father! Get my Father! Only he knows how to beat me properly!

> *The **Maid** rushes to do so; and bumps into **Rosencrantz** and **Guildenstern** who have entered during the beating, posing in background.*

Maid   Bastards!

Guildenstern   Ma'am! I beg your ...

Maid   Bullies, bastards, tyrants, oppressors, brutes, bloodsuckers!

Rosencrantz   I'm sorry, I ...

Maid   Malignant mutants, morbid, compulsive, obsessive woman-haters! Is destruction of our sex your only source of meaning and identity? Why else your contempt! Your mindless hatred of our very being? Your cheerful, unselfconscious, sadistic, ruthless, spectacular cruelty? You filthy, godless, drunken, vicious bastards!

Guildenstern   Ma'am, really ... !

Maid   All men are bastards! All men are rapists! Bullies, villains, bawdy bloody villains! Why can't you leave us alone? (*Punching their chests*) Leave us alone! Leave us alone!

> *The **Maid** runs out wailing. **Rosencrantz** and **Guildenstern** recover and compose themselves. Pause.*

Guildenstern   Interesting, gentle Rosencrantz.

Rosencrantz   Extraordinary, gentle Guildenstern.

*They notice **Ophelia** on the floor, and share a concerned look.*

*(If the **Interval** is placed here, blackout and music. If it is after the next scene, **Rosencrantz** and **Guildenstern** should gently lift **Ophelia** to her feet and help her off.)*

Scene 5

*The **Players** enter wearing masks, hats or wigs if the actors are doubling and need to be disguised. They could look like standard Shakespearean actors. They are doing an unusual and attractive voice exercise. **Horatio** follows them on admiringly, and claps when they finish.*

Player 1 Latest voice warm-up – we have to indulge these modern ideas.

Horatio Well, if that's the warm-up I can't wait to see the show.

Player 1 We aim to please.

Player 2 We aim to please too much sometimes; you are likely to find our exercises more interesting than our plays these days, Horatio.

Horatio Dissension?

Player 3 Ah yes, there has been much throwing about of brains ...

Player 1 The old argument, my friend. Our younger, greener members long to be provocative and challenging – I prefer to eat; and so eventually would they, I'm sure.

Player 4 Horatio, reason with him. The purpose of theatre is not merely to *please*?

Player 1 The more you please, the more people come ...

Player 3 Bums on seats ...

Player 2 But don't you want any brains in the heads above those bums?

Horatio Elitist theatre!

Player 4 So? So what?

Player 3 I want theatres full too – but I want theatres full of people who *like* theatre.

Player 2   If you try to please everybody, you end up with plays that bore the interesting theatregoers and then they stop coming!

Player 3   What's the point of attracting everybody to come, and then having theatres full of people who don't really want to be there?

Player 4   Watching actors doing plays they don't really want to be in?

Player 2   Plays so vapid and mindless that the only time the audience feels any real dramatic tension and excitement is when somebody forgets their lines?

Player 2   Musicals, domestic comedies ...

Player 3   'Physical theatre', performance art ...

Player 4   Mime! (*All groan*)

Player 2   Theatre is questions and answers, feeling the social pulse; looking into ourselves, exploring our own culture ...

Player 4   Theatre's about taking *risks* ...

Player 3   Horatio - reason with them.

Horatio   So the danger lurking in the simple goal of filling the theatre is that you lose could your committed audience ...

Player 2   *And* our good actors and writers, who give up in disgust and do something else. We lose *all* ways.

Player 3   We've been trying for two months to recruit another actor ...

Player 1   It's the *pay* that puts them off.

Player 4   Acting is a vocation, like – like priesthood! A real actor doesn't care about pay!

Horatio   Surely you must aim for balance – please and provoke and challenge at the same time ...?

Player 4   Compromise? Never!

Player 2   We played for Fortinbras last week – he threatened to withdraw his sponsorship if we said anything remotely anti-war.

Player 1   Well he's a soldier for goodness sake! We've got to eat! And what a feast he put on, Horatio ...

Horatio   I'm afraid all we've got for you is warmed-up leftovers from the wedding breakfast.

Player 3   All we seem to care about is keeping the sponsors happy.

Player 4   Caviar for the generals!

Player 1   Horatio, please don't encourage them – they'll be wanting *female* actors next.

Player 4   Well? And why not?

> *All laugh at **Player 4**.*

Player 1   I thought you wanted a discerning audience? Who would come to plays full of whores, do you think? And you, for one, would be out of a job! Come on lad, only men know how to portray women realistically on stage. That's surely one thing at least the world can agree on.

Horatio   Well, yes - look at Chinese Opera ...

Player 1   ... Kabuki Theatre. It would take years to train a woman to do it ...

> ***Hamlet** enters, all bow.*

Hamlet   Good, you're here. Now this play of yours, 'The Marriage Trap' – this is a new one?

Player 1   Our premiere tonight, my lord, in the King and Queen's honour ...

Hamlet   It's funny, I hope?

Player 1   Very, my lord.

Hamlet   Excellent. Now I have a scene here I want you to add. It's not at all funny so it'll be a great contrast ...

> *The **Players** are extremely alarmed.*

Player 1   A whole new scene, my lord?

Hamlet   Yes, that's all. Slot it in at the beginning somewhere. Now it's important you do it *big*, you know – (*He 'acts', very grandly, sawing the air with his arms*)

'You vile Uncle, who killed my father so you could marry my mother and be king yourself! Don't think I don't know, because I do! Ho ho! O, bloody bawdy villain! Remorseless, treacherous, lecherous, kindless villain!'

> *Pause*

Player 1   Ah ... very good, my lord. *(Appalled, he claps)*

Hamlet   It doesn't matter if you don't follow it, just get the words out – big and loud. But make sure you've got them laughing to start with; warm them up, relax them, you know – plenty of slapstick, grubby jokes, nothing subtle ...

Player 1   Schoolboy humour.

Hamlet   Exactly!

Player 1   (*Grovelling*) Of course we can fit your scene in – a great honour, my lord.

Hamlet   Right! The stables are free for rehearsal.

Player 2   (*As they go, to **Player 1***) But the play! You can't just chop it up and chuck in pieces from all over the place!

> The **Players** leave, complaining.

Hamlet   Action at last, Horatio!

Horatio   Yes my lord, but – what exactly do you hope to achieve by it?

Hamlet   Achieve? Oh Horatio, do but think how sweet a thing it is to wear a crown. The play's the thing wherein I'll catch the conscience of the king!

Horatio   My lord – forgive me for harping on – but are you sure that ghost was your father?

Hamlet   Of course!

Horatio   It's just that ...

Hamlet   Horatio, Horatio! As if I wouldn't know my own dear, dead – murdered – father!

> *He is emotional; he embraces **Horatio** who consoles him awkwardly.*
>
> *Enter **Polonius** and the **Maid**, ushering in **Ophelia** in sackcloth and a crown of thorns, bleeding, bruised, pale and fraught, concentrating heavenward with praying hands. She see the two men embracing, and concentrates harder. She is holding a bundle of **Hamlet's** letters and poems tightly.*

Polonius   Ahem. My lord, a word.

Hamlet   (*Taunting; his arm around **Horatio***) How now, Ophelia?

Polonius   I fear you have ... offended my daughter, my lord.

Hamlet   How do *you* know? You haven't been eavesdropping, have you?

Polonius   My lord ...

Hamlet   Pronounce!

Polonius   The Queen, your mother, in great affliction of spirit, hath sent me to you ...

Hamlet   Was she listening too?

Polonius   She desires ...

Hamlet   Desires? My mother desires?

Polonius   She desires to speak with you in her closet before you go to bed.

Hamlet   We shall obey, were she ten times our mother. But soft! What is that creature? *(Pointing to **Ophelia**)*

Polonius   Pardon, my lord?

Hamlet   That clown, that tart in tatters – or is it a lump of coal?

Polonius   Ah – very like, my lord.

Hamlet   No, a monster – some bird of prey?

Polonius   Bird of prey – very like.

Hamlet   *(Sniffs her)* Or a bag of compost?

Polonius   Um?

Hamlet   But now I must get drunk!

Polonius   Drunk, my lord?

Hamlet   Of course! We have a play to see! Whoever heard of watching a play sober! Come Horatio. (*Gives him a kiss to annoy **Ophelia**. **Horatio** is covered in confusion.*) Farewell, fools!

> ***Ophelia** hurls his letters at him with a wail; then pulls herself together and concentrates heavenward again. **Horatio** picks them up, concerned.*

Hamlet   Come, Horatio!

> ***Hamlet** and **Horatio** leave.*

Polonius   Oh what a noble mind is here o'erthrown! The Queen is quite right – the poor boy is mad; quite quite mad. Oh to see such talent wasted!

Ophelia, I was at fault – you must be gentle with him – you must make allowances; sensitive young men of ability and breeding, of fine and delicate parts, are very highly strung and most easily disturbed. Be warm therefore, be generous – give him love, compassion – no longer shun his company and we may yet calm his soul. You could have the life of our future king in your hands ...

Maid   My lord, I fear your daughter is also deeply disturbed ...

Polonius   Is she indeed? Well snap out of it. Neurotic bloody women ... Now, prepare her for the play girl. And for the last time get rid of that damn black thing!

> **Polonius** leaves. **Ophelia** is trembling, swaying and staring. The **Maid** embraces her, very upset. **Horatio** returns with the letters.

Horatio   Madam, I am certain Hamlet would prefer you to keep these ...

Maid   (*Holding **Ophelia** up*) Wouldn't it be more fitting for *you* to keep them?

Horatio   Ma'am, forgive his behaviour; he has – a lot on his mind ...

Maid   And he sends *you* to beg forgiveness? To smooth out his mistakes – to procure for him?

Ophelia   (*Viciously*) Pimp! Faggot! Fairy! (*Pulls herself together guiltily and prays again*)

Horatio   Simply – I would rather not see my friends unhappy, and if I can do anything ...

Maid   Please inform your lord that the Lady Ophelia doesn't give a damn for his happiness, any more than you give a damn about hers! She never wants to set eyes on him again – he is wiped from the face of this earth! Ophelia renounces all MEN from this day forth!

Ophelia   (*Crazed*) Yes! yes!

Horatio   All men? Oh my lady no ... !

Maid   Can't you understand? Look at her! She hasn't eaten or slept for days; she prays deliriously, screams for guidance, beats herself, cuts herself; her hair's falling out, her gums are bleeding ! She's in torment! And all because of your halfwit friend and his mindless cruelty!

> She rushes to catch **Ophelia** who is falling; **Horatio** is mortified

She fell into a sadness, then into a fast, thence to a watch, thence into a weakness, thence to a lightness and by this declension into the madness wherein she now raves, and I mourn for ...

Horatio *(Aside)* O this is the very ecstasy of love! *(To **Ophelia**)* Madam, take care. I will do as you say.

> *He bows, but before he can straighten up and leave, **Ophelia** has staggered over to him, and grabbing him for balance occasionally ...*

Ophelia *(Piously)*
Give me your pardon sir, I have done you wrong,
But pardon it as you are a gentleman.
You cannot help your nature; and I am wrong,
we are all wrong to mock you for it.
We should try to lighten each other's burdens
as you are trying to do for you beloved prince.
You are a good man, and I have sinned. Forgive my taunts.
Forgive my jealousy. Are we friends? *(She offers her hand)*

Horatio Friends?

> *They shake hands; **Ophelia** swoons and falls into him. **Horatio** is deeply troubled. She stands again.*

Ophelia Sorry. *(Getting her balance)* Why can't we be friends? We both love him. Both are rejected in our different ways.

Horatio My lady ...

Ophelia We are bound by a common torment -

Horatio We are both in torment, yes ...

Ophelia *(Elated)* My jealousy has gone, compassion takes its place! Once again my prayers are answered, and evil banished from my soul!

Horatio Oh ... good.

Ophelia Let us be friends, Horatio.

> ***Ophelia** clasps his hands; and swoons into him again.*

Horatio *(Catching her; anguished)* Ophelia ... !

Hamlet *(Off)* Horatio!

> ***Horatio** tries to transfer **Ophelia** to the **Maid** as **Hamlet** enters.*

Hamlet Horatio, what are you doing with that bag of bones? Drop it at once and explain yourself.

Horatio My lord, she fell ...

Hamlet Remember the words of Odilo of Cluny – 'to embrace a woman is to embrace a sack of manure.' Remember the filth that is covered by her white skin, Horatio ...

> *The **Maid**, who now holds **Ophelia**, hears this. **Ophelia**, back to her religious trance, doesn't.*

Horatio Hamlet, she loves you, she loves you still, but she is ill, she is hurt and upset ...

Hamlet Of course she is, that's the whole idea. Keep them guessing. Now – come and get drunk!

> *Horatio, hitherto fiercely loyal to his friend and future king, shows the first signs of losing patience with him. He hesitates, and then follows **Hamlet** off.*

> *The **Maid** is occasionally required to assist **Ophelia** physically during the following; she caresses her, weeping and moaning gently from time to time.*

Ophelia (*Piously, sweetly, elated*) Oh I am flooded with joy! I apologise to a fellow creature, banishing envy and bitterness from my heart, and am forthwith radiant with love! Ah, I am addicted to goodness!

> *She falls to knees suddenly, groaning, growling.*

O Hamlet! O my prince, my lord, my man, my demon-lover! You reject my love, and it comes back to me as poison, it eats away at me like acid! Oh, I am burning, I'm burning, I'm burning up inside! O, why do I crucify myself? No I can't bear it no, no – Oh lord, help me, help me endure, help me endure ...

> *A pause, as she gathers strength; then fiercely determined –*

I will not give up! I will not give up! This is the passion of the gods, of heroes, the ecstasy of saints! Would Cleopatra have given up ? Isolde? Juliet? Medusa? Delilah? Dido? Bathsheba? Judith? Boadicea? Helen of Troy? Would they have given up?

Oh no no no no no. I shall transform ... henceforth I will wear WHITE ... float, drift by him in white silk and muslin ... a garland of wildflowers speckled with dew ...

> *She sways and dithers round the room, in a parody of that other **Ophelia**.*

I shall be pale, luminous – I shall line my eyes with charcoal – lithe, graceful as a willow – *nothing* shall pass my lips but milk and royal jelly – I shall waft through these halls like a spirit, fragrant with musk and sandalwood ... I shall *fascinate* him!

And slowly growing in stature and dignity ...

Artists, scholars, poets and princes will travel the world to see me – I shall be Muse, icon, symbol of the age; ideal, anima – I shall pass into *myth!*

I shall be awesome, magnificent, I shall poison his dreams, haunt his days, eat away his heart! He will be dazzled! He will be devastated! He will *respect* me! He *will!*

*Long pause. The **Maid** slowly raises her head.*

Respect? Did I say respect?

Maid   Yes madam yes; you said respect, not love!

Ophelia   Odd!

Maid   No no; it's not his love you want!

Ophelia   But then – what is this pain? This burning?

Maid   Anger, madam. Fury that you have been so – humiliated!

Ophelia   Humiliated?

Maid   Abused, mistreated, bullied, ignored, sneered at, every day, every night, every hour – it's an endless suffering ... (*Sobbing*)

Ophelia   So this agony of longing is for nothing but – a sweet revenge?

Maid   Forget him, ma'am forget him.

Ophelia   (*Drained, flat*) He was my way out; my passport to the world; to the wild and dangerous world of men ... energy, freedom, excitement. Cowboys and Indians. Cut and thrust. I'm terrified I'll never get another; that I'll be condemned to stay here, down here, in the little, petty world of women, bitter and spinstered, no way out ...

But it's true. I don't want his love; I don't want *him.* Of course I don't love him. So why – what is this aching emptiness then? This yawning despair? Why do I feel as if something precious has been torn from me? What is it I think I've lost?

***Ophelia** collapses in a heap.*

Oh god! Dumped back down among the women. I've stopped burning. I'm just a pile of ashes. I am nothing.

Maid   Now see that noble and most sovereign reason like sweet bells jangled, out of time and harsh. That unmatched form and feature of blown youth, blasted with ecstasy. O woe is me, to have seen what I have seen, see what I see. *(She sobs)*

> **Rosencrantz** and **Guildenstern** *enter and survey the piteous scene before them. They carry a bunch of flowers and a clipboard; and carefully approach.*

Rosencrantz   Ah madam, vouchsafe a word with you.

Guildenstern   We heard you were out of sorts. *(Giving flowers)*

Ophelia   For me?

Rosencrantz   Do you know us ma'am?

Ophelia   Yes, you are fishmongers.

Guildenstern   Not us ma'am.

Ophelia   A pity; they are honest men; they treat their customers with *respect* ...

Rosencrantz   An honest man is one in a thousand ma'am.

Guildenstern   And a respectful one, one in a million.

Ophelia   True, true.

Rosencrantz   Madam, we'd like a word.

Ophelia   Words, words, words ...

Guildenstern   Concerning the prince.

Rosencrantz   That's why the Queen summoned us here.

Guildenstern   To find out what's up with him ... so ...

Ophelia   Absolutely out of the question!

> *She tries to get up and leave but staggers badly.* **R&G** *grab her in time.*

Guildenstern   *(To **Maid**)* You! Mead for three! Go!

> *The **Maid** leaves.*

Rosencrantz   Here, sit down.

Guildenstern   To tell the truth, we're bored with him too.

Rosencrantz We've had him up to here.

Guildenstern We're much more interested in *you*.

Ophelia What do you want with me? Don't touch me! I want respect, do you hear? No man touches me again!

Rosencrantz No man? But – we thought you were to be married …

Ophelia Ha! How can I consider the sacrament of marriage with a soul as vile as mine? I must remain a virgin or be forever damned.

Guildenstern You will enter a convent then?

Ophelia Well, I suppose; what else can I …? But do I have a vocation? How great a sin is it to enter a convent without one? You're educated men - what do the saints advise?

> *The **Maid** enters with mead; during the following **R&G** revive **Ophelia** with a few sips.*

Rosencrantz Now – nuns and virgins – this is an area of enquiry that has absorbed us considerably, Guildenstern.

Guildenstern It certainly has, Rosencrantz.

Maid Madam, you should rest now …

Ophelia No, wait! Quiet! Gentlemen?

Guildenstern Now let me see; virgins. The cult of the virgin didn't begin till the 13th century …

Ophelia Cult?

> *Ophelia becomes increasingly amazed throughout the following; and the **Maid**, more and more horrified.*

Rosencrantz The cult of Joseph as head of a holy family – 15th century …

Guilenstern Marriage didn't become a sacrament – till death do us part, and all that stuff, till – 1563?

Rosencrantz I think 4.

Guildenstern The best marriage in the eyes of God is one where the partners remain virgins. St Augustine.

Rosencrantz And St Bernard of Clairvaux gave – 86 sermons?

Guildenstern 87.

Rosencrantz 87 sermons on the Song of Songs, demanding we become inebriated with love, purple with passion – and at the same time, deny all physical desires.

Guildenstern And as for St. Theresa ...

Ophelia Oh! (*Shocked, she swoons again*)

Rosencrantz (*Catching her*) I don't think she's ready for Theresa, Guildenstern.

Guildenstern Right. Well – we had a problem with all that stuff, didn't we Rosencrantz?

Rosencrantz We found the church's obsession with chastity incompre-bloody-hensible.

Guildenstern Mass hysteria; a lunacy epidemic.

Rosencrantz Healthy desire contorted into a rather nasty form of sado-masochism ...

Guildenstern The basis of the aforementioned vocation.

Rosencrantz You see, while a nun is 'free', in a manner of speaking ...

Guildenstern ... *she is free in a system that despises women.*

Both Conundrum.

> Pause. ***R&G*** *nervously await her reaction.*

Ophelia More! More! Go on!

> *Encouraged,* ***R&G*** *get more excited, conspiratorial.*

Rosencrantz Ah, well –

Guildenstern We set about getting to the bottom of it.

Rosencrantz The University didn't know what we were doing ...

Guildenstern We snuck into the off-limits part of the library –

Rosencrantz And researched the meaning

Guildenstern The *real* meaning –

Rosencrantz Of 'Virginity'.

Ophelia Ah! And?

Rosencrantz We found a lot of things.

Guildenstern We found Adam's last will and testament.

Rosencrantz It said 'Don't believe Eve's version' (*They laugh*)

Guildenstern Eve didn't fall, she was pushed! (*Laughing louder*)

Ophelia (*Impatient*) But Virginity! Virginity, what does it mean!!

> *R&G pull themselves together, and become very serious, grand and mystic ...*

Guildenstern Virginity means – Independence. Being true to the self.

> *Pause.*

Ophelia True to the self??

Rosencrantz A true Virgin is a woman who chooses her own direction; who is submissive to no one, who is in charge of her own life, who allows *no one* dominion over her inner being ...

Guildenstern She trusts her feelings, and acts on them, and doesn't care what anyone says. She's strong, and honest, and brave. She's *free.*

Rosencrantz She is honest about her desires. She is free to take lovers, or reject them. NO one owns her. No one violates her integrity.

> *Ophelia gasps with delight; the Maid with horror.*

Ophelia O my. O my O my O my!!

Guildenstern So let us drink to Elizabeth the First. Powerful Virgin Queen of many lovers!

Rosencrantz And to Penthesilea, Queen of the Amazons! Who tore her lover limb from limb when he tried to steal her independence!

All 3 TO VIRGINS!!

> *They drink a toast. Ophelia, elated, paces about, her head spinning, full of questions.*

Ophelia But – how is it possible for a word's meaning to be forgotten like that? How can that happen?

Rosencrantz Easy. Rewrite history. Outlaw knowledge.

Guildenstern In 2,300 BC, the Chief Priest of Sumeria composed a hymn in the praise of God. Both the priest and the god were female. Forgotten.

Rosencrantz Women didn't see much use for men in those days.

Guildenstern They burnt us for sacrifices, ordered us about.

Rosencrantz But – By 500 AD, Christians had closed the last of the Goddess's temples. Sexual pleasure, outlawed; reproduction, dirty; prophecy, witchcraft. Virgins – of the old sort – no longer required.

Guildenstern Everything arse about face.

Rosencrantz And all forgotten – nearly. If it wasn't for us.

Guildenstern (*Indicating the horrified* **Maid***)* Can she be trusted? We could be burnt for telling you this.

Ophelia But – they must have been very evil times! It is *unnatural* for women to ... men are *naturally* dominant, so ...

Rosencrantz And fleas *naturally* bite you and give you the plague – does this mean we should sit back and let them?

Ophelia But it's women's nature to be mothers, homemakers, not ...

Guildenstern That's what they say – as natural as it is for a fish to live in water. Any woman who wants a different environment must be 'unnatural'.

Rosencrantz However – you don't have to force a fish to stay in water. Whereas to keep a woman in her so called 'natural' environment, the state has found it necessary to pass a stack of laws as long as your arm. Doesn't that make you suspicious?

Guildenstern To by *compelled by law* to live in a way that's supposed to come naturally?

Ophelia Then – then the laws must be changed. Women must change the law!

Rosencrantz How? The law says you're not allowed to vote!

Ophelia Aaargh!!

Guildenstern And be careful - being female means you're deviant before you start. Being a defiant female is *intolerably* deviant.

Rosencrantz Burning hurts.

> *Maybe at around this point they are becoming ever so slightly affected by the Mead*

Ophelia But – why do men still hate us so? They've got us where they want us, they've got power, we have none. Why do they still hurt us so much?

Guildenstern   Men have twisted women to fit their vision of 'ideal female' – and now they don't like the results!

Rosencrantz   'They clip her wings – and then get angry that she can't fly'. St Simone.

Ophelia   All men are monsters! Bastards and monsters!

Rosencrantz   Hey, steady on ...

Ophelia   Well of course *you* wouldn't agree.

Guildenstern   We're not monsters – we're just brought up to believe some monstrous things ...

Rosencrantz   Most men are decent, doing their best. They just carry this – this monster around with them ...

Guildenstern   Hate the monster, not the man.

Ophelia   O yes? And is there anything left to love?

Rosencrantz   Well; history's full of lots of women who thought so ...

Ophelia   But were they True Virgins? And tell me – if the hymen means nothing, how does such a woman *lose* her virginity?

> *Pause. **R&G** come close to her, and quietly intone.*

Rosencrantz   When she betrays her true self ...

Guildenstern   When she submits to others against her will ...

Rosencrantz   Follows rules she doesn't believe in ...

Guildenstern   Contorts her behaviour to please other people ...

Rosencrantz   Allows others to bully her – to own her ...

Guildenstern   Then she has betrayed herself. Her soul is polluted. She is defiled. She is no longer a Virgin.

> *Pause. **Ophelia** stands, suddenly horrified.*

Ophelia   Gentlemen; I am not a Virgin! Oh my god, I'm not a Virgin, I'm not a Virgin! What am I to do?

> ***R&G**, now slightly inebriated, grab **Ophelia** who is flailing about staggering, and hold her as firmly as they can.*

Guildenstern Calm yourself madam!

Rosencrantz True virginity need never be lost forever!

Guildenstern True virginity can be *regained!*

Ophelia O yes of course, yes yes I see. Yes of course it can!

Guildenstern This above all – to thine own self be true;
and it must follow, as the night the day,
thou canst not then be false to *anyone!*

A bell rings loudly for the start of the Play.

*(If the Interval is placed here, **R&G**, **Ophelia** and **Maid** freeze;
blackout. At the end of the interval, Scene 6 should begin with the
same freeze and the Bell again, and the action continues as below.)*

If the interval is not placed here, the action continues thus –

Scene 6

*As soon as the Bell is heard, the **Players** and the rest of the cast
enter noisily. **Polonius** goes straight to **Ophelia** to tell her off and
R&G back away. **Hamlet** joins **Polonius**, rather drunk.*

*In the background, the **Players** are setting up, and the audience
chatting, choosing seats, bowing to the **Queen** (and **King**).*

Hamlet Weren't *you* in a play once, at university my lord?

Polonius I was indeed. I played Prospero.

Hamlet Ah, Prospero! Doesn't he have a beautiful daughter?

Polonius A very *obedient* daughter, my liege. Beautiful, chaste *and*
obedient.

Hamlet Who married a prince? Ha! She's blushing! Come my Miranda,
join me in the back row.

Ophelia NO.

Hamlet No?

Polonius (*Laughs nervously*) I am to blame, my lord, I have given unclear
instructions ... Ophelia, it is now permitted –

Ophelia NO.

Polonius It is my command, Ophelia. (*Pulls arm up her back so she can't resist*) Go!

> *Raucous music and* **Player Mother's** *entrance announce that the Play has started – (see full description coming up below).*

> *At the same time* **Hamlet** *drags* **Ophelia**, *distressed and bewildered that her first attempt at independence has been thwarted so easily, into the 'audience'. He holds onto her firmly.*

> *We see her face throughout as she doesn't watch the Play, which should be done at an angle allowing us to see something of both 'audience' and* **Players'** *faces.*

> THE PLAY:

> *Raucous music through the first section which is a 'domestic farce'. (If you are working with minimum cast the* **Players** *wear the same masks or wigs as in the earlier scene to pretend they are the same four people; they also wear basic costume for their roles.)*

> **Player Mother** *enters with huge shopping bags, perhaps pots and pans around her waist; she is holding a 'baby' she feeds occasionally on false breasts. She improvises loudly throughout on the hardships of housekeeping etc. She stirs pots, flaps nappies, shirts; irons, brooms, mops in a frantic round while* **Player 4**, *on knees, dressed as a small girl, cries, screams, knocks things over and pesters* **Player Mother** *throughout. At the peak she is doing several things at once in a frenzy. She is a typical male caricature of a woman, which the 'audience' finds hilarious. (Apart from* **Ophelia** *of course, who isn't watching.)*

> **Player Father** *comes home; overalls, hard hat; bellows, orders her about; where's my dinner, etc. He lifts her shirt and 'fucks' her absentmindedly while she's stirring the soup; whacks the kids, etc. The 'audience' all find this hysterical too. Around the lifting skirt moment* **Hamlet** *does something particularly gross to* **Ophelia**, *and she shrieks.*

> *At this point,* **Player Mother** *could give* **Player Father** *'dinner' and while he sits and gobbles, deliver a cut version of Kate's last speech from 'The Taming of the Shrew' (... 'thy husband is thy lord, thy life, thy master', etc.) directed at the* **Queen,** *who highly approves, as they all do and clap loudly.*

> *Then* **Father** *yawns and puts a crown on.* **Hamlet** *is immediately*

distracted and loosens his hold on **Ophelia,** *who leaves the 'audience' and comes downstage, upset.* **R&G** *notice her leaving and sneak away to join her.*

(The conversation between **R&G** *and* **Ophelia** *happens while the rest of the Play continues thus, quietly, in slow motion mime; timed so that it is in its last phases when* **Ophelia** *screams**.)*

Mother *puts crown on. Lets in* **Player Lover.**
They smooch; then go each side of **Father.**
Then they pour poison into his ear. He dies.
Lover *takes* **Father's** *crown off, and puts it on his own head.*
Mother *and* **Lover** *embrace.)*

Rosencrantz Madam, you need not tell us what the lord Hamlet did – we saw it all.

Guildenstern It makes us angry too.

Rosencrantz We know exactly how you feel.

Ophelia How *can* you? How *can* you know? Two men! How can I trust two men who tell me that if I choose to lose my hymen I will not lose my virginity? Ha! I must be mad!

Guildenstern When men offer women 'help', always check their motives.

Rosencrantz I wouldn't trust a man as far as I could throw him.

Ophelia Well then!

Guildenstern But we're not men, you see. *(Pause)* We're sisters.

Pause.

Ophelia Oh.

Rosencrantz Both of us. Women. *(Pause)* So that's all right then, isn't it?

Ophelia I don't feel well ...

Guildenstern Now you know you can trust us!

Ophelia You're mad. You're both mad.

Rosencrantz No no no, we are, really. Look.

R&G expose themselves, one a brassiered chest; the other invites a glance down well elasticised trousers.

*Simultaneously:- the play reaches its Mother/Lover embrace scene and the dummy King 'faints' (or the real **King**, if you have one, stands); **Ophelia** screams** piercingly as the **Queen** (or **King** if there is one) yells –*

Queen Give the King light! Away!

All Lights lights lights!

*Confusion. **Hamlet** chases the **King** (or dummy King held by the **Queen**), calling him a murderer; **R&G** chase **Hamlet**, the **Queen** screams. 'Audience' eventually all run off. The **Players** watch bewildered from their stage. **Ophelia** spins about during all this and finally collapses, alone.*

Player Father What was all that about?

Player Mother Where did everybody go?

Player Lover We hadn't even got started!

Player 4 The show must go on!

Player Father No way (*Looking at **Ophelia**)* There's fewer than us in the audience.

*They leave. **Player 4**, dressed as a girl still, is left on stage alone. He panics briefly, then soldiers on.*

Player 4 (*Curtsies to **Ophelia**)* Madam. (*She lifts her head*) By way of apology for this interrupted entertainment, I hope you will accept my recital of a famous poem by A.E.Housman.

He recites with feeling, wiping away a tear at the end.

'The laws of God, the laws of man
She may keep who will and can.
Not I – let God and man decree
Laws for themselves and not for me
And if my ways are not as theirs,
Let them mind their own affairs.
Their deeds I judge and much condemn
Yet when did I make laws for them?
Please yourselves, say I, and they
Need only look the other way.
But no, they will not; they must still
Wrest their neighbour to their will,
And make me dance as they desire
With jail and gallows and hellfire.

And how am I to face the odds
Of man's bedevilment and God's?
I a stranger, and afraid
In a world I never made.'

> *Ophelia, delighted, claps: **Player 4** curtsies.*

Ophelia Bravo, bravo! ... 'The laws of God, the laws of man, she my keep ... ?

Player 4 '... who will and can'.

Ophelia 'She may keep who will and can ... Not I! Not I!'

Player 4 'Let God and man decree laws for themselves ...'

Ophelia '... and *not* for me!'

Player 4 Speak clearly and simply, stay relaxed, and in control. Make sure you understand *exactly* what you're saying, and then, suit the action to the word, the word to the action. Don't strive for effect, don't aim to please, don't doubt what you know is right. Suit the action to the word ...

Both ... the word to the action ...

Player 4 ... and then it must follow, as the night the day, that you cannot be false to *anyone*.

Ophelia (*Taking his hands*) Oh wonderful, wonderful girl!

Player 4 (*Indignant*) I'm not a girl! (*He takes his wig off*) I'm a boy! (*He runs off*)

> *As a bewildered **Ophelia** attempts to absorb this the lights go strange; there are frightening rumbles and ghostly noises; it gets darker and darker ...*

Ophelia Light! Light! Give me light! (*She collapses again.*)

> *Pause. **Horatio** enters, and sees **Ophelia**. He nervously picks her up and carries her to her bed and lays her down, sitting nearby.*

> *At the same time the **Queen** and **Polonius** enter the Queen's area and whisper conspiratorially. (The **King** – if you have one – may also enter and get into the **Queen's** bed.)*

Scene 7

Hamlet, drunk and angry, arrives. The **Queen** *pushes* **Polonius** *behind a curtain. (If there is a* **King***, he could snore occasionally.)*

Hamlet (*Aside*) I will speak daggers to her, but use none. Now mother, what's the matter?

Queen Hamlet – you have your father much offended.

Hamlet Mother – you have my father much offended.

Queen Come come, you answer with and idle tongue.

Hamlet Go, go; you question with a wicked tongue.

Queen Why, how now Hamlet!

Hamlet What's the matter now?

Queen Have you forgot me?

Hamlet No no no; you are the Queen; your husband's brother's wife; and – would it were not so - you are my mother.

Queen What have I done, that you dare wag your tongue in noise so rude against me?

Hamlet Sit down, woman! Oh most pernicious woman! You shan't budge till I set up a glass where you may see the inmost part of you.

Polonius sneezes.

What! A rat?

Hamlet punches the curtain; we hear a smash and cry of someone going through a window, and falling and crashing.

Queen O you mad fool!

Hamlet Was it the King? (*Looks out*) Him? What was he doing here?

Queen Oh what a rash and bloody deed is this.

Hamlet A bloody deed! Almost as bad, good mother, as kill a king and marry with his brother. (*Looking out*) Thou wretched, rash intruding fool, farewell! (*To* **Queen***)* I said sit down! (*He pushes her down*). You *disgust* me!

Queen What ...?

Hamlet My father! My father! He's still warm in his grave and you marry that – that festering dumpling! How could you! How could you post with such unseemly speed from that noble warrior, that paragon of animals, the saint that was my father, to this loathsome, lusting slob! And his brother! My uncle! For God's sake that's – that's incest! How can you share a bed with that tub of sweating lard? Grappling flabbily together, stewing in vile corruption – I'm nauseous just thinking about it! Have you lost your reason? You ageing harlot, look at yourself! You're a laughing stock! Oh shame, where is thy blush!

Sex – at *your* age? What are you thinking of? What are you – witches, vampires, devil worshippers? You should be strung up and stoned, the pair of you!

And worst of all, you incestuous and adulterate beast, this garbage you fondle nightly is your husband's murderer! O vile, unnatural! A murderer, a killer of my father, our *king*! You lewd, evil, polluted old SLUT!

> *The **Queen** calmly throws a small scarf round his neck and pulls it tight.*

Queen Sit, Sit! I must be cruel, only to be kind.

> *She forces him to sit. Perhaps she ties the scarf to a bedpost. Incapacitated, **Hamlet** chokes faintly through the scene.*

My dear, sweet, only son – I think there are one or two things you need to know.

First, your father. He was an ignorant bully, a cowardly cheat, a bloodthirsty killer, a thoroughly useless husband and a damaging and dangerous father – a fact which you sadly prove. He was *not* a noble warrior and saint – and why you should indulge in this post-mortem adoration when you couldn't stand him when he was alive, I simply can't imagine. Though I've heard 'tis common.

Second; yes, Claudius killed your father, with the full approval of myself and 90% of his tyrannised subjects. His incessant war-mongering, and in particular, his nasty habit of murdering other people's fathers, has brought us to the brink of disaster.

Third; Claudius is a man who could avert that disaster. He is wise, sensible, diplomatic, decisive – and by marrying him, he becomes King and can guide our state safely through these troubled times.

> ***St Joan** appears around curtain.*

St Joan Excusez moi ...

Queen Get out! Get out at once!

> *St Joan goes, startled.*

If I hadn't married him, *you* would have been King – and let's face it, this is what really gets up your nose. But a more pathetic, dithering, bullying, puritanical, evil-tempered arrogant little squirt of a sovereign I cannot imagine. Not to mention the plunge that would have meant in my *own* fortunes.

Fourth – I actually love this man dearly, and have done for years. It may come as a shock, little boy, but quite a lot of people over 30 fondle each other. Oh yes, Claudius and I take our clothes off, heave our misshapen, wrinkly carcasses into bed and HAVE SEX; on a fairly regular basis. We have the effrontery to desire each other and actually don't care that this upsets *you*. We make love in the bed, on the floor, in the bath, in the garden, on the beach, on the banqueting table – and we are inconsiderate enough not to give a *shit* what drivelling adolescents like you think. There. (*She releases him*)

Hamlet (*Croaking*) O mother, speak no more! You turn my eyes into my very soul …

Queen Now, instead of interfering in my personal life, which is none of your business, why don't you bugger off and try to sort out your own! Assume a virtue if you have it not! Killing your beloved's father is *not* a good start. We'll try to keep it quiet – in the meantime, you'd better lug the guts into the potting shed.

Hamlet O wretched state – O bosom black as death! O liméd soul, that struggling to be free art more engaged! Help, angels!

Queen Oh, get on with it! Oh God; now that silly girl will be wearing mourning for *another* two years!

> *The **Queen** leaves (followed unobtrusively by the **King** if necessary). Pause.*

Hamlet (*Devastated*) Why do women get so … emotional …

> *Hamlet leaves.*

> *Lights cross to **Ophelia**'s area; **Horatio** asleep on the floor, **Ophelia** waking.*

Ophelia (*Joyous*) Oh! What a rogue and peasant slave am I!
Is it not monstrous that that little actor, but in a fiction, in a dream of passion
could force his soul so to his own conceit that from its working all his visage

wanned;
tears in his eyes, distraction in his aspect, a broken voice,
and his whole function suited
with forms to his conceit. And all for no one! For Ophelia!
What's Ophelia to him, or he to Ophelia,
That he should weep for her! What would he do
Had he the motive and the cue for passion that *I* have? He would drown the stage with tears
and cleave the general ear with horrid speech ...
Oh, I'm so *hungry*!

> **Horatio** *has woken and heard the last few lines. He offers her an apple.*

Ophelia Oh! Hullo, Horatio! Oh yum!

> *She takes the apple and eats.* **Horatio** *gets up his courage.*

Horatio Madam, I must speak. You are betrothed to our future king ...

Ophelia (*Mouth full*) Except he wants me to join a nunnery; to ensure we can't indulge in sinful passions. I interpret this as a subtle clue that his affections lie elsewhere ... You're in luck, Horatio ...

Horatio O villain! Smiling damned villain! That one may smile and smile and be a villain!

Ophelia Horatio!

Horatio Ma'am – desire is as natural as breathing; love of a fellow creature can pitch the mind and soul from the mundane to the sublime ... how can God do anything but smile on a love that helps us reach Him?

Ophelia Even a love that ... (*whispering*) dare not speak its name?

Horatio I don't know what love is. How can something that feels like agony bear the name of love?
I only know that –
A lover's eyes will gaze an eagle blind.
A lover's ears will hear the lowest sound.
Love's feeling is more soft and sensitive
than are the tender horns of cockled snails;
love's tongue proves dainty Bacchus gross in taste.
For valour, is not love a Hercules,
still climbing trees in the Hesperides?
Subtle as a Sphinx; as sweet and musical
As bright Apollo's lute, strung with his hair.
And when love speaks, the voice of all the gods

make heaven drowsy with the harmony.
Never durst poet touch a pen to write
until his ink were tempered with love's sighs;
O, then his lines would ravish savage ears,
and plant in tyrants mild humility.
From women's eyes this doctrine I derive.
They sparkle still the right Promethean fire;
they are the books, the arts, the academes
that show, contain and nourish all the world;
Women! ... by whom we men are men!

Oh forgive me Ophelia! I adore you, I worship you! I have watched over you,
prayed for you, begged that bastard to treat you kindly!

Oh goddess, angel, my soul, my life! ... I see you ill and desperate – oh, the
pain ... oh forgive my shameful lust, my lewd imaginings! I will never speak
of it again. I shall leave the castle tonight!

> *And he sits on the bed, anguished, head in hands.*

Ophelia   But Horatio, I thought ... I thought ...

Horatio   Oh I am in a torment of longing and guilt!

Ophelia   You mean – all this time? Oh, Horatio!

Horatio   I never looked at another woman because I only had eyes for you!
Forgive me, forgive me, forgive me ... *(He sobs)*

Ophelia   *(To herself)* There is a tide in the affairs of women which taken at
the flood, leads on to fortune; omitted, all the voyage of their life is bound in
shallows and in miseries. Horatio – my dear, dear friend ...

> *Very slowly she moves to him and touches him; he flinches and
> moves away. Pause. She touches him again.*

Horatio   Madam, this is cruel!

> *She continues to console him, murmuring as if to a mistreated
> animal. Very, very slowly he responds. They move slowly into a
> phase of awed, dazed, mutual absorption, gazing into eyes, touching
> each other's faces wonderingly ... At this point the **Maid** rushes in
> distraught. They neither see nor hear her. Lights begin to dim.*

Maid   *(Waving **Ophelia's** original black garments)* Oh madam, prepare
for mourning once again ... Oh Ma'am your father, your father ...

> *She sees **Horatio** and **Ophelia** who are obliviously entering their
> first kiss. The **Maid** is appalled, and backs away clutching clothes,*

*backing into the ghost of **Polonius** who has appeared; the **Maid** is dumbstruck with terror.*

*Throughout the following, **Horatio** and **Ophelia** are oblivious and slowly more and more involved, eventually starting to take off items of clothing.*

Polonius *(In a ghosty voice)* Mark me Ophelia. My hour is almost come when I to sulph'rous and tormenting flames must render up myself ...

*Unseen, **St Joan** arrives from the other side.*

I am thy father's spirit, and, it seems, doom'd for a certain time to walk the night ... List, list, o list – if thou didst ever thy dear father love, revenge his foul and most unnatural murder ...

Maid O God! O no ... no no no ... !

*   **Polonius** *leaves as the **Maid** backs into **St Joan**.*

St Joan Please, please listen to me ...

*The **Maid** shrieks hysterically and runs, taking the mourning clothes with her, laughing insanely as she goes.*

St Joan Merde!

*   **St Joan** *considers **Ophelia** and **Horatio** and thinks the better of it, and leaves, complaining in a French accent. Lights dim on the couple who are now seriously involved. The **Maid** and ghosts are wailing in the background.*

Scene 8

*All goes quiet. Pause. Morning birdsong. A ray of dawn light lands on the couple in the bed. **Ophelia** (wearing underwear) wakes and murmurs to **Horatio**.*

Horatio Must I be gone? It not yet near day ...

Ophelia You must go and live, or stay and die.

Horatio That light is not daylight, I know it, I; it is some meteor that the sun exhales to be to me this night a torch bearer, and light me on the way back to my room ... therefore I'll stay – I need not yet be gone ...

Ophelia   Let us be taken then – let my father kill us!

Horatio   I am content, if you would have it so ...

Ophelia   No, silly; *go*!

Horatio   If it is your will ...

Ophelia   You must, you know you must; begone, away!

>   *Horatio is dressing.*

Horatio   Shall I compare thee to a summer's day? Thou are more lovely ...

Ophelia   Sweet man, sweet, lovely man! Begone!

Horatio   I will think of you every minute of the day; I must see you every hour ...

Ophelia   I'll see what I can do, but please, go! We will be discovered!

Horatio   Ophelia, what is to become of us? We are star-crossed, we are doomed ...

Ophelia   How do you know we are doomed?

Horatio   Male intuition.

Ophelia   Tomorrow, maybe. But today, right now, we are very, very happy. (*Kiss*) Now go. No, no tears.

>   *She takes a distinctive handkerchief from his pocket and dabs his face.*

Horatio   That handkerchief did an Egyptian to my mother give; tis true – there's magic in the web of it – (*Giving her the handkerchief*) Keep it. Keep my tears, to remind you I am yours.

>   ***Ophelia** hides The Handkerchief in her cleavage. One last kiss, and **Horatio** goes, furtively. **Ophelia** turns to us, triumphant.*

Ophelia   At last! I am a Virgin!

>   ***St Joan** appears, weary.*

St Joan   Excusez moi ...

Ophelia   Oh!

St Joan   Can you see me?

Ophelia   Angels and ministers of grace defend us! Be thou a spirit of health or goblin damned? Bring with thee airs from heaven or blasts from hell ...?

St Joan Can you hear me?

Ophelia Yes!

St Joan Will you *listen* to me, and not interrupt, or run away panicking halfway through what it is I have to say?

Ophelia Yes; yes I'll listen. Stay, illusion!

St Joan Oh, at last! I will be brief and clear. (*She gets out her notes*) I have not long. Now. You had a king, who was - no forget that bit. There is a man, Fortinbras whose father was killed by ... no, never mind. (*Throws away her notes*) Brevity is the soul of wit. Listen; this is all that matters now. There is an angry army marching this way at this very moment, who aim to kill you all. This is clear?

Ophelia This is clear. Who is Fortinbras? Who are you?

St Joan You must tell the king. You must mobilise! You must defeat this foe or you will be overwhelmed! There. This is the message I am sent to give you. At last I have given it.

Ophelia Who are you?

St Joan My name is Joan. Joan of Arc. When I was alive no one would listen to me either – not till I heard my voices; *then* they took notice. But even then, all they were interested in was sainthood, miracles, whether I was a virgin. My mission was urgent – I had armies to organise! Yes, it's tough for a woman to get people to listen.

Ophelia Armies?

St Joan I am a soldier.

Ophelia A soldier? You pretended you were a man?

St Joan Never! God forbid! Joan the Maid, the Maid of Orleans.

Ophelia And they accepted you, in the army? I'm astounded.

St Joan Accepted me? I *led* the army, girl. One of my voices, St Margaret, was a monachoparthenist, however.

Ophelia A what?

St Joan She entered the monastery, as a man. The better to resemble Our Lord.

Ophelia She looked to Christ? Not Mary?

St Joan Oh, Our lady is – well, a lady; but Christ is *God*. And she was made a saint, thereby. And you. Married? Betrothed?

Ophelia I'm not sure that I want to be married.

St Joan Then you will be a nun. Bravo!

Ophelia Oh no.

St Joan A woman alone? And not a nun? Cherie, women have been burnt alive for less. Pray for guidance, child – or like me, you may not live to see your 20th birthday ...

Ophelia I will pray, I'm determined to find a way.

St Joan I like you. Most girls are soft and soppy things – but you – *(She clenches her fist)*. So I will give you some advice. When your prayers are answered, trust your voices. Listen to no one else. The Church is just the Church – it can make mistakes; terrible, terrible, tragic mistakes. But your voices never will. I will never forget that it was the Church that handed me over to the Inquisition.

> *The light is getting brighter.*

The sun! I go. You remember my message?

Ophelia Oh yes, yes ...

St Joan Remember, remember, remember me ...

> *She leaves.* **Ophelia** *considers, and looks towards* **Mary***.*

Ophelia 'The Church can make mistakes.' And you were certainly one of them. You! You nearly ruined my life, you know that? All this time, I've looked up to you – and – you don't know anything! You haven't *lived*.

Ask me! Go on, ask me; anything you like. What do you want to know? I bet you're dying to know! *(She waves **Horatio's** handkerchief at **Mary** tauntingly)*. How can you be wise, unless you've been *through* things? How can you have any idea what's good, or bad? Or even if there are such things? I bet you just believed what everybody told you! Just like me! Well, listen! People make mistakes. The *Church* is just people – the Church can make mistakes! You've GOT to think for yourself!

You've got a funny look on your face. I suppose – I don't suppose they've got you all wrong too? I wonder – what kind of a virgin are you???

> **Ophelia** *moves right up to* **Mary** *(aside, out of the light, or offstage; she is not involved at all in the following action, and no one is aware of her, or she of them)* **R&G** *come on from different*

entrances, frantic.

Both Thank God. I've found you!

Guildenstern The place is in confusion, dear Rosencrantz.

Rosencrantz What on earth is going on, dear Guildenstern?

Guildenstern Hamlet has killed Polonius. Laertes wants to kill him. Horatio is looking demented and the Queen is in a rage.

Rosencrantz And Ophelia?

Guildenstern She will be distraught, poor lady ...

Rosencrantz Look where she comes ...

*The **Maid** enters, in **Ophelia's** mourning clothes, mad; her face obscured somewhat by the veil.*

Guildenstern How now, Ophelia?

Maid Your beauteous majesties; good morning. Allow me to introduce myself! I can make bread, clean birds and fish, sift, cook, launder, make beds, spin, weave French purses, embroider, cut wool and linen cloths, put new feet in socks – I can kill and butcher a pig, salt meat, sow, reap, glean, winnow, grind and store grain, brew ale, make pots, hammocks, bedrolls, curtains, mend rag rugs; trade, barter, keep household accounts; keep and care for hens, cows, pigs and other livestock; grow vegetables and herbs; make medicines and potions for all manner of ailments. I am expert in husband and childcare; and highly skilled in the arts of service to young women of noble birth.

I have a mistress – oh, I have a mistress second to none in mastery of French, music, dancing, flower painting, embroidery and the backboard. Oh I am fulfilled! My cup runneth over! I am fire and air!

*Cheerfully singing, as **R&G** sob quietly.*

And I've got seven children at home
I've got seven children at home
What a joyous noise they make
Hey nonny nonny

I get home from work, I cook the tea
My husband comes home and bullies me
We're a jolly, normal family
Hey nonny nonny

Seven at home and one one the way
Life's a joyous holiday
I love my job and my piddling pay
Hey nonny nonny

I love washing nappies
I love washing nappies ...

> *This refrain continues as a miserable wail as she runs to the exit,*
> *leaving with an insane, hysterical laugh.*

Rosencrantz (*Sobbing*) We've lost her. We knew she was on the edge.

Guildenstern We thought we'd got to her in time.

Rosencrantz We must now look to ourselves. Where do we stand in this madhouse?

Guildenstern Are we still employed?

> *Laertes enters, wild.*

Laertes Hamlet! Hamlet! Coward; father-murderer! Where are you? (*To R&G threatening*) Where is he?

> *R&G stutter and mumble that they don't know, as the **Maid** re-*
> *enters, still in **Ophelia's** gear, followed by the **Queen** (and **King**),*
> *and carrying a large bunch of weeds, laughing.*

Maid What vegetables shall we have for tea? Everyone eat their greens please; everyone eat their greens, no waste, no waste, I'm not made of money.

(*to **Rosencrantz***) Here's carrots for you – eat them up or you won't see in the dark. (*wagging finger*) Eat, eat!

(*to **Guildenstern***) Here's onions for you – help fix that sniffle, curl your hair. Yes they will, don't answer back!

(*to **Laertes**, who is stunned*) And silverbeet for you, full of iron, make you grow strong; Come on, eat it. Eat it! I'm not telling you again, EAT IT! You've got to be strong, Betty, you've got to be strong, you've got to be strong ...

> *Suddenly sad; to herself*

What are women *for* mummy? Menstruation, defloration, pregnancy, childbirth, lactation, menopause. Let her have children till she dies. That's what she's for.

And suddenly, seriously, to the audience:-

If thou didst ever hold me in thy heart
absent thee from felicity a while
and in this harsh world, draw thy breath in pain
to tell *my* story.

And to the others, mad again:

Now where is that maid of mine. Have you seen her? Girl, where are you?
Perhaps if I called her by her name, do you think she'd come? If I was a little
kinder? Rosalind! Rosalind! Where are you? Oh she's lost, she's lost. I
must find her ... Fare you well my dears, fare you well ... Where are you sweet
maid? Where are you? ... O woe is me, to have seen what I've seen, see what
I see!

She runs off, wailing.

Laertes O heat dry up my brains! My sister, my sister! Hamlet, what have
you done to my sister?

*He runs off, bellowing for **Hamlet**.*

Queen *(To **R&G**)* Gentlemen, I charge you – find my son before Laertes
does! Disguise yourselves as nuns; there are bands of pilgrims walking to
Jerusalem – join them – here's money for your journey ... God speed! God
speed!

__Queen__ exits weeping. Pause.

Rosencrantz Nuns?

Guildenstern Walking – to *Jerusalem*?

Rosencrantz Yeah, right!

*They look at the money, each other; think; idea! They enter
Ophelia's area and start choosing and changing into some of the
frocks Polonius left for her.*

Rosencrantz I'm sure she wouldn't mind.

Guildenstern She has no mind left to mind with.

__Ophelia__ returns, still in underwear, and sees them changing.

Ophelia Oh, hullo!

Rosencrantz Ophelia! How did you ...?

They are confused, wondering how she could have taken her clothes off, recovered and got back so soon.

Guildenstern Are you – alright?

Ophelia Wonderful! I'm absolutely wonderful!!! And you really are women!

Rosencrantz Shhh!

Guildenstern Shhh!

> ***R&G*** *continue changing throughout the following, take off false moustaches, put lipstick on each other, brush hair out etc. In spite of actually being women, they're not practised in the art of it, and should end up looking very gawky and unconvincing.*

Ophelia And I've got a thousand questions!

Rosencrantz Fire away.

Ophelia WHO is SHE? (*Pointing to* **Mary**)

Guildenstern Oh dear. She changes. She changes all the time. Or rather, she is *changed*, to suit the times.

Rosencrantz No one had much to say about her till 431AD – declared Mother of God.

Guildenstern Immaculate Conception ...

Rosencrantz 1884.

Guildenstern Assumed into Heaven ...

Rosencrantz Not till 1950. Not many people know that! For a few centuries she was a powerful Queen. The Queen of Heaven. Bossy.

Guildenstern Then she became the bride of Christ.

Rosencrantz No wonder men are so confused ...

Guildenstern Then the private sweetheart of monks and sinners, the antidote to love on earth.

Rosencrantz Next she was meek, mild and skint – obedient to son and husband. Mrs Joseph; her indoors.

Guildenstern Psychologists declare her a female archetype; a perfect woman.

Rosencrantz Beware – wherever there's a celebration of a 'perfect woman', you can be sure *real* women are having a hard time.

Guildenstern There is more to heaven and earth than is found in your psychology, Ophelia …

Rosencrantz Or is she a sleeping goddess?

Guildenstern The heir to the true virgins, true daughter of the ancient pagan pantheon?

Rosencrantz Will she wake one day and insist on joining the male Trinity?

Guildenstern And then – perhaps …

Ophelia (*Gasping*) You mean – up there with them? *Four* of them?

Rosencrantz There is nothing either good or bad but thinking makes it so …

Guildenstern So – who is she? Take your pick.

Rosencrantz Better still, ask *her*. *She* knows who she is.

Ophelia I have been asking – but she seems shy. I'm not surprised – I've been very rude to her …

Guildenstern It'll take time - keep trying.

Ophelia I'm afraid of making God even more angry than he is already …

Guildenstern Eh? Oh, you mean the earthquakes, eclipses, the ghosts? Banish this superstition, Ophelia – the world's upheavals are not caused by the wrath of God –

Rosencrantz It's merely the conjunction of Jupiter, Mars and Saturn in the 40th degree of Aquarius. No mystery.

Guildenstern Astrology 210.

Ophelia (*Laughing*) This is all too much for me – the world has gone quite mad! Though if this be madness, there is method in it!

R&G remember her recent insanity, and exchange looks.

Guildenstern Ma'am – for many women madness is but a sane response to life's restrictions and absurdities …

Rosencrantz Mad women, ma'am, are often the sanest of us all …

Guildenstern The full moon drives women sane, not crazy.

Rosencrantz We thought we were mad once, didn't we, Guildenstern?

Guildenstern We did Rosencrantz. We wanted to go to university.

Rosencrantz They said – you're mad. All that unnatural mental activity will destroy your delicate nervous systems ...

Guildenstern Your ovaries will dry up. Your wombs will cave in.

Ophelia But you didn't care. You dressed up as boys and went! You plucked the apple of forbidden knowledge!

Rosencrantz Ophelia – there are thousands of us!

Guildenstern We dress up to learn, to write, to get published ...

Rosencrantz To join monasteries, go to sea ...

Guildenstern Be lawyers, doctors, avoid marriages ...

Rosencrantz Lead armies, run countries ...

Guildenstern Become Pope!

Rosencrantz There's at least four others in our Alchemy tutorial!

Ophelia A woman Pope!?

Guildenstern Pope Joan! She only got discovered when she had a baby!

Ophelia Oh brave new world that has such people in it!

They dance around the room together.

Oh, that reminds me! St Joan! Joan of Arc came to see me – she had a very important message for the king – an army is on its way to destroy us all. Will you tell him when you next see him?

Pause. ***R&G*** *think* ***Ophelia*** *has gone mad again.*

Guildenstern (*Carefully*) Ophelia, it will take a long time to get over your father's death.

Rosencrantz And even longer to forgive Hamlet for killing him.

Guildenstern Be gentle with yourself. A true Virgin can survive anything.

Ophelia (*Shocked*) My father? Hamlet killed my father?

She stands dazed.

Rosencrantz Ophelia, we have to go.

Guildenstern Have a bit of a lie down, eh?

Rosencrantz She's quite sane north northwest; when the wind is southerly she doesn't know a hawk from a handsaw.

Ophelia (*Wildly*) Hamlet killed my father! I shall cut his throat in the church!!

Rosencrantz Quickly Guildenstern, the coast is clear.

Guildenstern Farewell, dear lady. May Ishtar watch over you.

> *R&G leave, rapidly and nervously. Pause.*

Ophelia Hamlet? Hamlet killed my father?
Now I could drink hot blood, and do such bitter business as
The day would quake to look on!
O come you spirits
that tend on mortal thoughts; unsex me here;
and fill me, from the crown to the toe, top full
of direst cruelty. Make thick my blood,
stop up the access and passage to remorse
that no compunctious visitings of nature
shake my fell purpose, nor keep peace between
th'effect and it. Come to my woman's breasts,
and take my milk for gall, you murdering ministers –
Oh bloody, bawdy villain!
remorseless, treacherous, lecherous, kindless villain!
Oh, vengeance!

> *Through the following, she dresses in a mix of the men's gear that R&G have left behind, including a hat.*

Why, what an ass am I! This is most brave,
That I, the child of a dear father murdered
must, like a sailor, unpack my heart with
words, and fall a'cursing like a politician!
Fie upon it. Foh! (*She is now dressed and would pass for a young man*)
Suit the word to the action.
About my brains.

> *Suddenly she sees/remembers the **Maid's** love potion, thrown to the floor in Scene 1. She picks it up ... there is a tinkle of the same magic-music, perhaps. She has an idea.*

Ah, cupid! Wicked bastard of Venus; your time has come.

> *The sound of a crowd wailing sadly begins off stage; as it gets louder **Ophelia** hides where she can see and hear. Enter **Queen**, wailing loudly, and **Laertes**.*

Queen   One woe doth tread fast on another's heel, so fast they follow.
You're sister's drowned, Laertes!

Laertes   Drowned? O where?

> *During following, two cloaked figures bring on the covered body of
> the **Maid**.*

Queen   There is a willow grows aslant the brook
that shows his hoar leaves in the glassy stream;
therewith fantastic garlands did she make
of crowflowers, nettles, daisies and long purples
that liberal shepherds give a grosser name,
but our cold maids do dead men's fingers call them.

Laertes   (*Impatiently*) Yes! Yes!

Queen   There, on the pendant boughs her coronet weeds
clambering to hang, an envious sliver broke;
when down her weedy trophies and herself
fell in the weeping brook. Her clothes spread wide
and mermaid-like, awhile they bore her up
which time she chanted snatches of old lauds
as one incapable of her own distress,
or like a creature native and imbued
unto that element; but long it could not be
till that her garments, heavy with their drink,
pulled the poor wretch from her melodious lay
to muddy death.

Laertes   You mean; you just *stood* there – and watched her drown?

Queen   (*Sobbing*) Laertes, alas, I cannot swim! (*She moves off*)

Laertes   (*Following*) You actually saw her fall in, listened to her singing,
and *watched* her *sink*?

> *The **Queen** and **Laertes** leave. **Ophelia** comes out of hiding.*

Ophelia   Who *are* you?

> *She goes to the body and lifts the shroud. We see an unrecognisable
> face, maybe covered with slime or seaweed; she has no idea who it
> is.*

Ugh, what a mess.

> *She brushes aside some of the debris, but still can't recognise her.*

A woman. Just a woman. And just this morning this face was washed, teeth brushed, hair combed. Lips spoke, sang, kissed her babies ... these eyes wept.

Alas, poor woman.
Oh, what is a woman.
If her chief good and market of her time
be but to serve, and breed? A beast, no more.
Surely he that made us, gave us not
that capability and godlike reason
to fust in us, unused?
(Covering her up again)
Ah, we are such stuff as dreams are made on
and our little life is rounded with a sleep ...

> *More wailing off.* **Ophelia** *hides again.* **Hamlet** *enters followed by* **Laertes.** **Hamlet** *falls over the body, wailing.*

Hamlet   Ophelia! My angel! My love, my love!

Laertes   *Your* love! I loved her more than you!

Hamlet   You! 40,000 brothers could not, with all their quantity of love, make up my sum!

> **Horatio** *enters, shattered. He moves quietly to the body and weeps.*

Laertes   I loved her more!

Hamlet   You did not!

Laertes   I did so you murdering bastard!

Hamlet   Did not!

Laertes   Did so!

> *They fight, trying to punch each other.*

Horatio   Stop it, stop it you mad fools! If you loved her, at least show her *body* some respect!

> **Horatio** *goes back to mourning.* **Ophelia,** *making some attempt to hide her face with the hat, comes forward.*

Ophelia   *(Trying to sound male)* My lords! *(Bows awkwardly)* I bring an important message from the king.

> **Hamlet** *and* **Laertes** *are united briefly by mutual homophobia.*

Hamlet Laertes – dost know this waterfly?

Laertes Certainly not.

Hamlet Sir, a gentleman's hat is for his head, not his face.

Laertes You have a name, pixie?

Ophelia Ah – Oh – ahem - *Osric*, at your service. (*Bows*)

Hamlet We humbly thank you, Osric. And your message? Stand straighter, man, you're an embarrassment to your sex.

Laertes And the hat, please!

Ophelia It's hot, my lord.

Hamlet No it's not – it's cold.

Ophelia Ah yes - it is quite cold. I – my lord ... the king requests that Prince Hamlet and Laertes settle their differences in a duel.

Hamlet I do believe its voice has yet to break!

Laertes I beseech you, remember! (*Pulling her shoulders back roughly*)

Ophelia My lords – may I inform the king that you will obey?

Laertes I will win, therefore you may.

Hamlet On the contrary, I shall win, therefore yes, you may. Laertes, prepare to meet your maker. Farewell, fairy. Come Horatio, help me prepare.

     Hamlet *goes;* **Horatio** *ignores him and goes back to mourning.*

Ophelia (*Looking after* **Hamlet**; *with a feeling this is the last time*). Goodbye my lord, goodbye. Adieu, adieu. (*She sees* **Laertes** *leaving*) Oh - my lord Laertes – a moment.

Laertes What is it, faggot?

Ophelia Sir – I knew your sister.

Laertes What of it?

Ophelia But an hour before her death, she begged me a favour.

Laertes Yes?

Ophelia She begged me give you this.

She holds up the phial of love potion; a tinkle of magic-music again

Laertes What is it?

Ophelia A deadly poison. A lep'rous distillment. She bought this unction of a mountebank. One drop is fatal. One scratch from a blade dipped herein - lethal. The blood possets like curd, the body enveloped in a loathsome crust ... Your sister said she knew you'd have a use for it. And that is all I know.

Laertes Oh brave and clever sister! Good Osric, wear your hat where you like! Here, for your pains.

*He gives her a purse of money and leaves, calling for **Hamlet**.*

Ophelia (*Ecstatic at her acting success*) One scratch, and Hamlet will adore the next creature he sees. Who will it be? The King? The Queen? A donkey? O revenge is sweet! Hamlet in love, Hamlet's heart breaking! This I must see!

But what's this. (*She opens the purse*) Oh, money! My own money. My *own* money!

*She turns to follow **Hamlet** and **Laertes**, but then notices **Horatio** still weeping over the body.*

Ophelia Now cracks a noble heart. (*She gives him The Handkerchief*)

Horatio Thank you, thank you, sir.

***Ophelia** leaves. **Horatio** mops his face and speaks lovingly to the body.*

Goodnight sweet princess, and flights of angels sing thee to thy rest.

*As he mops, **Horatio** recognises the Handkerchief, and gasps.*

The Handkerchief!

*Puzzled, he looks after **Osric**. Then he looks more closely at the body. On more intimate inspection he realises it isn't **Ophelia**. Hope rises. He gasps, and rushes off after her.*

*Pause. The **Maid's** ghost, now clean and tidy, slowly emerges from the shroud, and re-covers the 'body' tenderly. She admires her pristine ghost clothes.*

One or two voices start offstage, followed by more and more, as the whole court falls in love with each other; this develops into a mass offstage improvisation.

Various Voices (*Offstage*) I love you! I love you! I love you! I adore you! (etc.)

> *The Maid exits to investigate.*
>
> *The lovefest then degenerates into jealous scenes:-*

Various Voices (*Offstage*) Leave him alone, he's mine! I love him more than you! You cheat! (etc.)

> *This in turn degenerates into screaming, sound of swords clashing, fighting and wounding noises.*
>
> *Soon this develops into extended dying noises. As we listen to the whole court expire, **Ophelia** enters, still dressed as Osric.*

Ophelia My stupid brother! He put in the drinks! They're all crazy with love and mad with jealousy! All of them!

> *The last groans are heard, and the **Maid** enters. **Ophelia** cannot see her.*

Out, out, brief candles!

> *She weeps, and the **Maid** goes and comforts her, **Ophelia** unaware.*

Oh Daddy, Daddy. I will miss you so, you old bully. Daddy what shall I do? I'm all alone, all alone ...

> *Pause, as **Ophelia** sobs. Then there is the sound of trumpets, and hammering on doors. Voices yell 'Open up, open up' etc, in strange Scandinavian accents.*

Oh no, the army! Joan's army! I'll be raped. I'll be beaten, I'll be burned alive!

> ***Ophelia** conceals herself and the **Maid** watches, and the noise subsides. The **Players** suddenly rush on, startled.*

Player 1 Well that was easy. They were nearly all dead before the army got here!

Player 2 And here's another one. (*Looking at the **Maid's** 'body'*)

Player 3 Do you think it was some kind of pact?

Player 4 I thought they were going to kill us. Why didn't they kill us?

Player 1 Kill actors?

Player 4 We'd better be careful, we're already one short.

Player 2   They'd have no one to entertain them at the victory feast, to immortalise their great triumphs.

Player 3   And they still might kill us if we don't put on a good show.

Ophelia   (*Emerging nervously*) Excuse me, I've heard you may be looking for another actor?

All   (*Turning to her eagerly*) Yes!!

Ophelia   Well then, may I join you?

> **The Players** *look her up and down; she passes muster so far.*

Player 1   Speak a speech, I pray you.

> **Ophelia** *panics briefly – then noticing* **Player 4** *remembers his poem. She delivers the first two lines as Osric)*

The laws of God, the laws of man,
She may keep who will and can ...

> *She struggles to remember; then abandons Osric and delivers the rest of the poem as herself – to her own self being true!*

Not I, let God and man decree
laws for themselves, and not for me.
and if my ways are not as theirs
let them mind their own affairs.
I, a stranger, and afraid
in a world I never made.

> **Player 4** *looks curious; they all clap.*

Player 1   Excellent, excellent. The pay's lousy, the work's hard, we're always on the move.

Ophelia   Fine! (*All are delighted as she shakes* **Player 1's** *hand*) Osric!

Player 1   You get a month's trial, Osric. (*Others shake hands*) Here, learn the part of Lucky. (*Giving her the script of 'Waiting for Godot'*)

Player 4   You know, I think you could pass as a woman. What do you think? Do you think he'd make a good woman?

> **Ophelia** *and* **Player 4** *exchange looks. The others all study her.*

Ophelia   Hmm. Would I make a good woman? I'm not sure what that involves, exactly. But – I'm prepared to try!

Player 1   Excellent. Now, do you know how to take a bow?

Ophelia tries, and is tutored by the *Players*. As she gets it right, *Horatio* rushes on calling her name. *Ophelia* and *Player 4* quieten him, as the rest of the cast rush on too, and all bow together.

THE END

{The Play Press}

... specialises in publishing plays, both to preserve a range of quality scripts and to make texts more accessible for rehearsal and study. The Play Press is interested in all types of playscript and any other performance related work.

Fold by Jo Randerson & **shudder** by Pip Hall
Mapaki by Dianna Fuemana & **Frangipani Perfume** by Makerita Urale
Fresh off the Boat by Oscar Kightley and Simon Small
Horseplay, Trick of the Light, Flipside by Ken Duncum (with VUP)
Ophelia Thinks Harder by Jean Betts (with WPP*)
Revenge of the Amazons by Jean Betts (with WPP*)
The Collective by Jean Betts (based on "Brecht & Co" by John Fuegi)(with WPP*)
The Misandrist by Jean Betts
Camelot School by Jean Betts
Baghdad, Baby! by Dean Parker
Awhi Tapu by Albert Belz
The Cape by Vivienne Plumb
Kikia Te Poa by Matthew Saville
The Mall by Thomas Sainsbury

*The Women's Play Press

Frontwomen by Lorae Parry
Love Knots by Vivienne Plumb
Lashings of Whipped Cream by Fiona Samuel
Cracks by Lorae Parry
The Case of Katherine Mansfield by Cathy Downes
Eugenia by Lorae Parry (with VUP)
Ka Shue (Letters Home) by Lynda Chanwai Earle
Vagabonds by Lorae Parry (with VUP)
Red Light Means Stop Vivienne Plumb (ed)
Foh Sarn (Fire Mountain) & Ka Shue (Letters Home) by Lynda Chanwai Earle
Farewell Speech by Cathy Downes, adapted from the novel by Rachel McAlpine

All available from:-

The Play Press
P.O. Box 27436, Wellington 6141, New Zealand
www.playpress.co.nz : stuff@playpress.co.nz